THE GOOD LIVING GUIDE TO
HEALING SOUPS

THE GOOD LIVING GUIDE TO
HEALING SOUPS

NOURISHING SOUPS, STEWS, AND BROTHS

SUSAN CROWTHER & JULIE FALLONE

New York, New York

Text copyright © 2025 by Susan Crowther and Julie Fallone
Photographs copyright © 2025 by Julie Fallone

All rights reserved. No part of this book may be reproduced in any manner without the express written consent of the publisher, except in the case of brief excerpts in critical reviews or articles. All inquiries should be addressed to Good Books, 307 West 36th Street, 11th Floor, New York, NY 10018.

Good Books books may be purchased in bulk at special discounts for sales promotion, corporate gifts, fund-raising, or educational purposes. Special editions can also be created to specifications. For details, contact the Special Sales Department, Good Books, 307 West 36th Street, 11th Floor, New York, NY 10018 or info@skyhorsepublishing.com.

Good Books is an imprint of Skyhorse Publishing, Inc.®, a Delaware corporation.

Visit our website at www.goodbooks.com.

10 9 8 7 6 5 4 3 2 1

Library of Congress Cataloging-in-Publication Data is available on file.

Cover design by Kai Texel
Cover photo by Julie Fallone

Print ISBN: 978-1-68099-934-1
Ebook ISBN: 978-1-68099-982-2

Printed in China

DISCLAIMER:
The recipes in this book and their potential benefits are intended as purely anecdotal, and no medical claims of any kind are made. We are not prescribing, diagnosing, nor recommending. We make no claims to curative powers.

It is important to note that consuming healing soups should not be considered a replacement for conventional medical treatment. For any and all health concerns, and before embarking on any lifestyle changes, consult a healthcare professional. Discuss with them any possible contraindications or potential interactions between herbs and medications to ensure that ingredients are safe for individual consumption.

Dedications

Susan:
To Marcia, the Compost Queen. More.

Julie:
To my mother-in-Law, Julieta Robledo Fallone. She opened her house and gave me her kitchen without blinking. She also gave birth to the love of my life.

Contents

Our Soup Stories	1
Soup as Medicine	5
Stock vs. Broth . . . Huh?	10
Healing Soup Recipes	21
Immune System	23
Nervous System	50
Circulatory System	68
Digestive System	92
Respiratory System	117
Endocrine System	140
Integumentary System	163
Soup Sides	183
Specialty Ingredients	215
References	*217*
About the Authors	*227*
Metric Conversions	*228*
Index	*230*

Our Soup Stories

Susan

As a young girl, I played a cooking game called Mish Mash, combining food together in playful ways to create weird dishes. Mish Mash was about curiosity—making mistakes and learning from them. The game evolved into a way of cooking that inspired my first book, *The No Recipe Cookbook* (Skyhorse, 2013).

My mother Marcia is the true pioneer of Mish Mash, known for her specialty, Compost Soup. Mom would clear out the freezer, dump several containers into a pot, heat them up, and taste. Whatever ethnic flavor it most resembled, she would then accentuate with that region's seasoning. The results were a clean freezer and a hearty supper! Marcia's motto in life? *It's perfectly good.*

Playing in the kitchen remained a lifelong pursuit, and I found myself at the Culinary Institute of America (CIA). As a CIA grad, people think I'm a big shot. When they ask me what is my favorite thing to cook, the answer always disappoints. Folks expect fancy dishes like Beef Wellington or Baked Alaska; but alas, my heart belongs to soup.

Soups are wonderfully suited to Mish Mash! They are unpretentious and universal, accommodating every culture or budget. Soups are valuable, rich in whole foods, herbs, and spices. They are simple to make and delicious for days. And yes, soups can be healing, thanks in large part to their base, the humble stock.

Bone broth is a hot foodie trend, but soup stock, as it's commonly known, has been around for ages. Stock is nothing fancy, but don't tell that to celebrity chefs like the renowned Thomas Keller, owner of two 3-star Michelin restaurants, who touts the virtues of "clean stock." Keller washes the stock bones first, then blanches them (pre-boils), then rinses them, and *then* makes the stock. He actually prefers to blanch the bones twice, for the ultimate clean stock. "You peel your vegetables," Keller says. "You skim everything all the time. You want everything cleaned, and that means removing what you do not want in your stock." Keller believes that if you've got a perfect stock, then you can make a perfect soup.

As I play in my own kitchen, I consider Thomas Keller's philosophy: *only put ingredients in the stock that you would actually eat.* I, respectfully, and maybe a little disrespectfully, disagree.

To make stock is to celebrate the untouchables—those un-eatable scraps filled with potential. Our book *Pickle & Ferment* describes the healthy microbiome living on the surface of plants. Nutritional treasures are lurking in leaves, skins, roots, and bones. All too often the medicinal parts are the very parts that chefs peel off, toss aside, and scrub clean. Cooking isn't antiseptic. Sure, it's important to be neat, but we're talking about a kitchen, not a laboratory. Julia Child would practice the five-second rule; and if it's good enough for Julia, it's good enough for me.

Soup stock, Mish Mash . . . cooking in general is never perfect. I shut the front door on your elitist ways, Chef Thomas. We honor the scraps around here, giving them purpose and loving their gifts. To quote Thomas Keller's own mentor, Master Chef Roland G. Henin: *Scraps equals soufflé.* (Chef Henin says it more colorfully, and we shall pardon his French.)

As you begin to explore this book and play in your own kitchen, remember the wisdom of Marcia and her Compost Soup: It's perfectly good.

Julie

My mother, Linda, was an elegant and refined cook. She could make soup out of a picked-clean chicken carcass and an empty refrigerator. She was the queen of getting one more meal out of things, which usually led to soup. It is something that I always remember her doing. The DuCharmes were a very frugal family. If something that was usually thrown away could feed you again, why not make soup out of it? My in-laws think I'm a crazy person when I save a carcass or a bone from a holiday meal, but I know there's always one more meal to be gotten. I hear her voice whisper in my head. I am my mother's daughter.

We had a cast-iron Dutch oven that looked like a witch's cauldron, and this was what my mom used to make soup. In my memories, I would watch my mother make soup out of thin air without a recipe as if casting a spell. Strange frozen wrapped bundles would be pulled out and thawed in the sink. Any vegetable tossed into a freezer could reappear magically in a stock.

Almost 100 percent of her soups started with chopped garlic in olive oil.

I was pretty young, but one of my first memories about a recipe was thinking, what could such a tiny amount of garlic contribute to the soup? I remember asking about the bay leaf in the stock. What does the bay leaf even do? This is something I still question. I would watch in fascination as she added every dash, pinch, and sprinkle and ask why. We were a family of six, but soup was never made for just six people. Instead, it was always closer to eighteen or twenty-four people. Leftovers were frozen to appear at a moment's notice months later. Because mom baked her own bread, "Soup with Bread" was a regular on our weekly menu. Soup was like the loaves and the fishes. Soup was frugal. There was always enough for everyone. Nothing went to waste.

I firmly believe there is a soup-making gene. I can make soup with my eyes closed. If I have a day off, just blast some music, give me a sharp knife and a refrigerator full of random ingredients and I am in my happy place. I know soup-making is hereditary because I see my mother's soup DNA in my children. My son, Max, can make a clean-out-the-refrigerator soup and people will ask him for his recipe. My daughter, Claire, makes a white bean, sausage, and kale soup that I have recurring dreams about.

My mother often got her inspiration from the *New York Times* cooking section. We did not live in Manhattan or always have access to all the ingredients, but we lived and ate an aspirational New York City lifestyle. Her soups adapted to fit what we had available in the kitchen. She often tweaked to replace an ingredient we couldn't afford or was out of season. Yet, without fail, every soup she touched was successful. . . . Well, except for the "Brazilian Black Bean Soup" incident, which we don't discuss.

I miss that childlike wonder of standing on a chair, arms on the counter, watching my mom make soup. But then I watch my children cook and feel it all over again.

Soup as Medicine

"Let food be thy medicine and medicine be thy food."
—Hippocrates

Stone Soup

A beggar is penniless and hungry, wandering through the woods, when he comes upon a clearing and in there, a house. He reaches down and picks up a stone in the yard, approaches the front door, and knocks upon it.

"Who's there?" a woman's voice asks.

"Good evening, ma'am," the beggar replies. "I am a wayward soul, traveling without food nor money. However, I possess a magical stone. By simply placing this stone into a pot of water, it will produce the most delicious soup you have ever tasted. If you would be so kind, I would be happy to show you how it works, sharing my magic and, thereby, creating a magnificent meal for your supper."

"That is most interesting! I would like to see this, indeed. Do come in!"

The woman invites the man inside. She brings out her large cauldron and fills it with water. She places the cauldron on the stove while the man cleans the stone. As the water comes to a boil, the man gently places the stone into the caldron and gives it a stir. "Now we wait!" he exclaims.

After a few minutes, the man declares, "What a lovely soup we shall soon have! I should not like to impose upon you longer than necessary. Perhaps if you have a couple potatoes handy, we could add them to the soup, only to hasten its thickening and shorten my imposition."

"That's very thoughtful of you!" she replies.

A few minutes pass. The man observes, "Oh my, look at those fine carrots in the corner over there, growing their tops and becoming hairy. What a shame to have them go rotten. Why not toss them into the soup?"

"A wise observation, good sir!" she replies.

A few more minutes pass. The man remarks, "You know what goes well with carrot and potato? The rich flavor of onion, that's for sure. Yes, some onion would make the soup grand, indeed."

"What a delicious suggestion!" the woman replies.

They continue chatting. The man remarks, "What is soup without a fine bone? Preferably one with a good lot of fat on it."

"I have the perfect bone!" cries the woman, rushing off toward the icebox. Next, the man concludes, "And to top it off, some herbs and spices—as important to a soup as a conductor is to an orchestra."

"How delightful a metaphor!" shrieks the woman, tossing salt and garlic gaily into the cauldron.

Soon the soup is finished, and the man and woman sit down to a steamy bowl. "How I love a couple slices of warm bread slathered with fresh butter to complement my soup."

"But of course!" chimes the woman. "Where are my manners? Would you care for some wine?"

They dine together, and it is, indeed, a magnificent soup. Afterward the man thanks the woman kindly for her hospitality and makes his leave. Abruptly the front door opens, and the woman rushes out after the man, calling, "Wait! You forgot your magic stone!!"

"And so I have! Dear me, I wouldn't want to lose this precious parcel! Warm thanks extend to you and your hospitality. Good night!"

The man, whistling, tosses the stone over his shoulder as he continues down the road.

> *Without proper diet, medicine is of no use. With proper diet, medicine is of no need.*
>
> —Ancient Ayurvedic proverb

Healing Power of Soup

Stone Soup illustrates the placebo effect and how magic plays a role in cooking. The placebo effect is a psychological phenomenon where people experience positive outcomes from a benign substance or treatment—

one that has no active ingredient. Placebos are influenced by factors like expectation, conditioning, and hope, and they demonstrate the powerful role the mind plays in health and healing. But despite the placebo effect, soup does stand on its own merit, offering medicinal healing benefits and maybe even a dollop of magic. Soup heals holistically, in mind, body, and spirit.

Soup heals physically. Our appetite often suffers when we're sick, and soup delivers easy nourishment. Soups are packed with nutrients from vegetables, beans, grains, meats, fish, herbs, and spices, all of which support the immune system and replenish depleted nutrients lost in illness. Soups tend to be gentler on the stomach than heavier foods, which is helpful when digestion is sluggish. Soups' high fiber stimulates elimination and helps to detoxify the body.

One of soup's great mysterious powers lies in its liquid, called stock. Stock is a great way to rehydrate. Staying hydrated is one of the ways the body can more effectively fight off illness. Soup stock is a rich source of electrolytes, the essential minerals needed to regulate body fluids and transmit electrical impulses throughout the body, and it may be better tolerated than sports drinks or water. Stock's warmth soothes a sore throat, settles the stomach, and relaxes the muscles. Soup steam helps break up mucus, clears nasal congestion, and relieves sinus pressure and pain. It can also have mild anti-inflammatory effects, helping to relax muscles and soothe cold symptoms. Soups' softened ingredients are easy to swallow for inflamed throats.

Soup heals mentally. When we're sick, we often feel bad and want to be comforted. Soup's nutrients help facilitate brain function (mood regulation) when we are unable to receive these from other food sources. Savoring a warm bowl of soup can be a soothing and satisfying sensory experience (try saying that phrase three times really fast). The soup-making process itself can promote mindfulness. Focusing on the ingredients, preparation, and flavors can keep us focused on the present, thus reducing anxiety. The soup aromas can evoke nostalgic memories and offer serenity.

Soup is also a healthy spiritual choice, in that it embodies responsible living. Soup honors conservation, repurposing leftovers and using excess vegetables (the ones waiting patiently in the veggie bin!). Vegetable scraps are utilized for healthy soup stocks. Soup is simple to prepare, the original "one bowl" recipe. Soup is economical, an inexpensive option that can help reduce financial stress. Soup is practical; one batch keeps for days and often gets better in the fridge. It is simple to eat, simple to clean up, and simple to take on the go.

The logic and simplicity of soup is perfect for a hectic, chaotic world. Soup is humble, honoring the food that creates it. In mind, body, and spirit, eating soup is a logical part of a healthy lifestyle.

"Eat your soup before it gets cold."

—Every Jewish mother

Chicken Soup

Chicken soup, the icon for medicinal soup, is consumed throughout the world in every culture. In Traditional Chinese Medicine (TCM), chicken soup is believed to have warming properties, used to nourish the body and strengthen the immune system. Since the Middle Ages, Jewish culture has embraced chicken soup for its medicinal purposes, often incorporating it into dietary practices during illness. Chicken soup with matzo balls is known as "Jewish penicillin." The Greek physician Galen prescribed chicken soup for various ailments like migraines, leprosy, and constipation. Vietnamese pho, a noodle soup with chicken stock and spices, is considered a restorative dish.

Chicken soup's reputation is built upon helping colds and flu. Like most soups, chicken soup is an easy way to get important micronutrients, macronutrients, and fluids when lacking an appetite. Chicken stock provides fluids and electrolytes that help the body fight off infections and ward off symptoms. Soup ingredients are well-cooked and therefore easy to digest, which is important when a person is sick.

Chicken is a good source of proteins. Proteins break down into amino acids, the body's "building blocks" that play crucial roles in various functions, including muscle growth, cell and tissue repair, and neurotransmitter production. Amino acids and peptides (short chains of amino acids) provide an energy boost that stimulates immune function.

Chicken is also high in the protein tryptophan, which converts to serotonin, enhancing mood and encouraging rest.

Chicken is an excellent source of the amino acid cysteine, which can help thin mucus. Chicken soup may contain a number of substances with beneficial medicinal activity including an anti-inflammatory mechanism that could ease the symptoms of upper respiratory tract infections. Some even include further anti-inflammatory ingredients like ginger. Chicken soup inhibits something known as neutrophil chemotaxis. A neutrophil is a specialized immune cell. Basically, white blood cells behave differently after consuming chicken soup, resulting in added anti-inflammatory activity.

Chicken soup is rich in collagen and hyaluronic acid, promoting healthier skin. It is nutrient-rich with vitamins B, C, and K, and minerals such as calcium, phosphorus, magnesium, and iron. These help our bodies fight off viruses and recover from illness more quickly. Calcium and phosphorus can contribute to strong and healthy bones, reducing the risk of osteoporosis.

Wherever it is consumed, in whatever culture, and whichever ailment, chicken stock has earned its rightful place as a main course at the healing soup table. Therefore, we've included a variety of chicken soups in this book for a variety of ailments!

Stock vs. Broth... Huh?

All soups have liquid. The ideal liquid is called "stock." It's also referred to as "broth." Most folks use these terms interchangeably. The differences between stock and broth are in their main ingredients. Stock is generally made from bones, and broth is generally made from flesh (meat). Stock is simmered for hours and creates a hearty nutritional liquid, while broth is a lighter version, usually prepared within an hour. Both stock and broth can be plant- or animal-based. Vegetable stock is a kind of "vegetable tea"—water infused with vegetable scraps, herbs, and spices. Because of how it's prepared, vegetable stock would technically be a broth. To make matters even more confusing, the term "bone broth" has become quite faddish; but technically, because of the use of bones and how it is prepared, bone broth would be considered a stock.

Huh?

There's a reason why the food service industry calls them "stockpots." Therefore, for simplicity and common sense, we will refer to all liquid bases, regardless of whether they are bone, flesh, or plant-based, as stock. With all of this hullabaloo, why even go through the trouble to make stock? Because stock is the foundation from which all of soup's healing benefits emerge.

Animal stock is associated with collagen, a structural protein found in skin, cartilage, and bone. As stock simmers, the collagen in connective tissue breaks down into gelatin and various other health-promoting amino acids such as glycine and glutamine. These substances are beneficial to hair, skin, and nail growth. Collagen may also be effective at reducing pain and stiffness and improving joint function.

Gelatin is the most abundant protein in stock and offers many health benefits. Gelatin can soothe the gastrointestinal (GI) tract, aiding digestion and absorption of nutrients. Gelatin binds with water to support the healthy movement of food through the intestines. Gelatin and other

amino acids found in stock may have therapeutic potential in inflammatory bowel disease. It may also be beneficial for injury prevention and tissue and tendon repair. Gelatin is rich in amino acids glycine and proline, which can support joint health, skin elasticity, and digestive function. Glycine and proline can support joint health and reduce inflammation, supporting conditions like arthritis. Gelatin can also help improve skin elasticity and hydration, promoting a healthy and youthful complexion.

Stock may help strengthen the gut-brain axis—the neurological "superhighway" that connects the gut to the brain—thereby affecting both mental and digestive health. The small intestine is the primary site for nutrient absorption, and it is also the first line of defense in our immune system. If the gut barrier becomes damaged or leaky, this can disrupt immune function. Glycine and glutamine may be protective, supporting intestinal barrier function, and increasing intestinal immunity and microbial diversity. The amino acid glycine has multiple functions in the body, including supporting healthy sleep patterns and reducing insomnia. Glycine helps regulate the internal body clock and lower body temperature to prepare us for sleep.

Before making healing soups, we need to make healing stocks. The following recipes are both animal- and plant-based. There is a lot of wiggle room in terms of substituting ingredients, but these basic guidelines will get you started on the right track.

Let's start taking stock!

Notes for Stock Recipes

Water. As with all cooking, remember the motto: the better the ingredients, the better the outcome. Always use GOOD water from a well or spring-fed source. If using tap water, filter it.

Bones. We've included a basic soup stock recipe. While stock is typically made from chicken, beef, or fish bones, feel free to use any combination of animal bones. One helpful technique is to freeze bones from meals. When a full bag of bones is saved, then make stock.

Vegetables. Stock can be made with vegetables only. Remember to save vegetable scraps and use them for stock. More explicit instructions are in the Vegetable Scrap Stock recipe (page 19).

Salt. Soup stock is unsalted. Seasonings come later, in soup recipes.

Worry. Don't worry too much about it. Cook stock when you have time. Make a batch and then freeze it in quarts for future soups. Homemade stock is absolutely worth the extra effort but *only* if time allows and you enjoy doing it. Otherwise, there are many high-quality organic stock options available in supermarkets and natural foods stores.

Basic Soup Stock

Use this rich, long-simmered stock in soup recipes or simply enjoy it in a cup. (Remember drinking bouillon? Like that.)

Makes 3 quarts (about 12 servings)

Ingredients:
4 pounds raw animal bones: beef, chicken, pork, lamb, etc. or any combination*
2 tablespoons vegetable oil
1 gallon cold water + extra, if desired

Optional:
1 onion, unpeeled and chopped
2 carrots, unpeeled and chopped
2 celery stalks, chopped
1 whole garlic bulb, cut in half, crosswise
2 bay leaves
Several fresh thyme sprigs
1 tablespoon whole black peppercorns

Directions:
Preheat oven to 450°F. Line a baking sheet with aluminum foil. Place bones on baking sheet and drizzle with oil; toss to coat, and arrange in an even layer. Roast until bones are lightly browned, about 30 minutes. Using tongs, transfer roasted bones to a large stockpot. Add cold water. Bring to a gentle boil over medium heat for about 30 minutes, skimming the foam and fat often. Reduce heat to low; simmer, uncovered, skimming surface occasionally, for at least 8 hours. If using optional ingredients, add these now, and continue simmering for a few more hours. More water can be added, if the stock reduces too quickly.

(Continued)

Place a fine-mesh strainer over a large heatproof bowl. Carefully ladle stock through the strainer. Using tongs, discard bones. If using optional vegetables, pour the vegetables and remaining liquid into the strainer, pressing with the back of the ladle on the solids to extract any remaining broth. Compost the vegetable scraps.

Stock may be used immediately, refrigerated, or frozen. If consumed as is (think "bouillon" or "bone broth"), season to taste with sea salt; otherwise, leave the stock unsalted for use as a base in recipes. If storing, let the stock cool completely at room temperature. Skim off any foam or fat that rises to the surface. Store the stock in an airtight container in the refrigerator for up to 1 week or freeze for up to 3 months.

Notes:
Stock may be prepared in a slow cooker. Place all ingredients in a slow cooker or Instant Pot, cover, and cook on Low for 24 hours. Skim occasionally, and then finish using the directions above.

---

* If bones are left over from a meal, skip the roasting.

Basic Vegetable Stock

Vegetable stock takes less time to cook than the animal version. It's lighter in flavor and color, but just as nutritious. Feel free to add other vegetable scraps, such as mushrooms, potatoes, tomatoes, etc. Experiment with different herbs and spices to create unique flavor profiles.

Makes 3 quarts (about 12 servings)

Ingredients:
¼ cup olive oil
3 onions (1 pound), unpeeled and chopped
5 carrots (1 pound), unpeeled and chopped
5 celery stalks, chopped
1 whole garlic bulbs, unpeeled, cut in half, crosswise
2 bay leaves
Several fresh thyme sprigs
1 tablespoon whole black peppercorns
1 gallon water

Directions:
Heat the olive oil in a large soup pot over medium heat.

Add the onion, carrots, and celery. Sauté for 10 minutes, stirring occasionally until softened and lightly browned. Add the garlic, herbs, and spices and stir for a few minutes, allowing the pungent flavors to release.

Pour in the water and increase heat to high. Bring *just* to a boil, and then immediately reduce heat to low. Simmer gently for 1 to 2 hours. Remove the pot from heat. If time allows, let the stock cool for about an hour before straining.

(Continued)

Place a fine-mesh strainer over a large heatproof bowl. Carefully ladle the vegetable stock through the strainer, pressing with the back of the ladle on the solids to extract any remaining stock. Compost the vegetable scraps.

Let the stock cool completely at room temperature. Skim off any foam that rises to the surface. Store the stock in an airtight container in the refrigerator for up to 1 week or freeze for up to 3 months.

Note:

Vegetable Scrap Stock

Another great way to make stock is from vegetable scraps. These are all the ends, leaves, skins, and bits of vegetable that are usually thrown away or composted. It is utilization at its finest!

Onion and garlic skins (skins add flavor and color)
Carrot stubs
Celery ends
Potato peelings
Green bean tips
Parsley/herb stems
etc.

Generally, if it is part of a vegetable, use it! First make stock, and then use the cooked scraps to feed the animals or compost bin.

Vegetable Scraps to Avoid

Celery leaves (they create a bitter flavor)

The Brassica family—broccoli, cabbage, and turnips—create strong, sulfur-like flavor. Use these when making Brassica soups

---

** Nightshade leaves: NEVER cook or eat leaves from potatoes, tomatoes, peppers, or eggplants. Nightshade leaves contain toxic substances.

Healing Soup Recipes

Some Notes to Get Started

Healing soups differ from regular soups in that their focus is on health benefits; therefore, the recipes reflect this, using specific ingredients and procedures.

The best ingredients yield the best results: buy organic products; choose local sources; visit farm stands; and grow gardens!

Nutrition is optimized in several ways:

- Soup stock instead of plain water
- Extra herbs and spices to heighten medicinal benefits
- "Superfoods"—nutrient-dense foods that contain an above-average amount of vitamins and minerals per gram
- Fresh herbs vs. dried
- Locally sourced, heritage, and wild-caught animals vs. commercial products
- Whole grains vs. "white" refined, e.g. basmati vs. white rice
- "Good" sugars—unrefined, whole vs. processed, etc.
- Sea salt vs. iodized salt
- Tamari vs. soy sauce
- Gluten-free vs. wheat options
- Einkorn wheat vs. commercialized hybridized wheat (see page 185 for information on einkorn)
- Herbs and spices are used specifically for their health benefits. For instance, black pepper can enhance the absorption and effectiveness of other herbs due to its compound called *piperine,* the primary alkaloid found in black pepper. Piperine can help increase the absorption of certain nutrients, including curcumin from turmeric, beta-carotene, and iron. This means the body can better utilize these

compounds for their intended benefits. Piperine can help inhibit certain enzymes that break down nutrients, allowing them to stay in the bloodstream longer and have a greater impact.
- Soups are pureed to thicken, instead of thickening practices that add starches, roux (made with refined wheat flour), etc. These thickeners add empty calories (calories that provide no nutritional benefit) and may exacerbate digestive ailments.
- All savory soups can use either meat or vegetable stock interchangeably. If a soup needs to be vegetarian, use vegetable stock.
- Recipes strive to use readily available ingredients in the United States. Ingredients that might be considered exotic or rare are left out in order to keep the soups accessible to the average consumer.
- Specialty ingredients are listed on page 215.

Immune System

The immune system is the body's defense system, made up of cells, tissues, and organs. Its main function is to stay vigilant against invaders and eliminate them. Invaders can be pathogenic microbes like bacteria, viruses, and parasites (harmful germs). They can be toxins. Invaders can also grow inside of us as abnormal cells (cancer, autoimmune responses). Invaders are called antigens. When antigens enter the body or are recognized, the immune system activates.

The immune system responds to invaders in two main ways: the innate immune response and the adaptive immune response. Innate immunity is the body's first line of defense, providing a rapid but general response to pathogens. Adaptive immunity is a slower, more targeted response that develops over time and can remember specific pathogens. Specialized cells, such as macrophages and neutrophils, engulf and destroy. Lymphocytes produce antibodies that target and neutralize invaders. Once the immune system has encountered and eliminated a particular antigen, it develops memory cells. These cells retain information about the invader and can quickly respond to future encounters, providing long-lasting protection.

The immune system is tightly regulated to ensure that it does not overreact and cause damage to healthy tissues. This regulation involves a balance of pro-inflammatory and anti-inflammatory responses. Autoimmune diseases happen when the system itself malfunctions, mistakenly attacking its own healthy tissues. The immune system can also overreact to harmless substances, leading to allergic reactions such as asthma. A healthy immune system can distinguish between "self" and "nonself."

In addition to its protective functions, the immune system also plays a role in tissue repair and wound healing. When tissues are damaged, immune cells help to clear away debris and promote the growth of new cells. This process is essential for healing wounds and preventing infections.

The immune system's effectiveness is influenced by various factors, including genetics, nutrition, and lifestyle. A healthy diet, regular exercise, and adequate sleep can help to boost the immune system's function. Conversely, factors such as stress, chronic illness, and certain medications can weaken the immune system, making individuals more susceptible to disease. The immune system is constantly working to protect the body from harm and maintain a state of balance. A weakened immune system leaves the body vulnerable to infections, illnesses, and even the body's own malfunctions. It is the silent guardian that keeps us healthy by fighting off threats both from outside and within.

Traditional Chicken

There are hundreds of chicken soups, from every culture and region across the world. An entire cookbook could be dedicated solely to chicken soup! This recipe provides a traditional basic chicken soup recipe, one that combines several herbs from different regions. Ingredients can be substituted freely, based on geography and personal taste.

Chicken soup is most known as a healing remedy for common colds and flu. The star of chicken soup is its stock. Chicken stock, made by simmering bones, provides essential amino acids that are crucial for immune cell function and body maintenance—helping to build and repair body tissues. The warm liquid soothes a sore throat and breaks up excess mucus.

Chicken soup is a great vehicle for consuming herbs and spices. Ginger, a potent anti-inflammatory and antioxidant, helps eliminate free radicals—unstable molecules created during metabolism. Free radicals can damage immune cells. It also possesses antibacterial and antiviral properties, which can aid in combating infections. Garlic is full of antimicrobial and anti-inflammatory properties, as well. Rosemary is an oral disinfectant. Thyme is a rich source of vitamin C, which helps boost immunity. Oregano is a powerful immune stimulant that is used for reducing coughs and bronchitis. Star anise is known to help calm the nerves and reduce flatulence. Because of its effects on colds and flu, chicken soup may be a useful healing aid in the treatment of viral infections such as Covid, RSV, and other respiratory ailments. And like all soups, chicken soup provides nourishment and comfort!

(Continued)

Makes 8 servings

Ingredients:
3 tablespoons olive oil
1 large onion, thinly sliced
2 carrots, thinly sliced
3 celery stalks, thinly sliced
6 cloves fresh garlic, chopped
2 tablespoons fresh ginger root, peeled and grated
1 star anise pod
1 teaspoon cayenne pepper
1 pound boneless chicken breasts or thighs, cut into chunks
6 to 8 cups chicken stock
2 tablespoons freshly squeezed lemon juice or raw apple cider vinegar
Sea salt and fresh-ground black pepper, to taste
1 teaspoon fresh rosemary, finely chopped
2 tablespoons fresh thyme, finely chopped
2 tablespoons fresh oregano, finely chopped

Optional:
Thin slices of hot pepper for extra heat

Garnish:
Fresh parsley, chopped

Directions:
In a soup pot, heat olive oil over medium heat. Sauté onion, carrots, and celery for 5 minutes. Add the garlic, ginger, star anise, and cayenne. Sauté for another 5 minutes. Add the chicken, stock, and lemon juice. Simmer for 30 minutes. Add salt and pepper to taste. Just before serving, remove the star anise and add the fresh herbs.

Notes:
Adjust the amount of stock, depending on desired thickness. Less stock will create a thicker soup, more like a stew.

To make a heartier stew, add ½ cup of brown rice when adding the stock. Simmer for about 45 minutes, until the rice is soft and tender.

Miso

Miso is the stuff of legend: In Tokyo, traffic controllers are purported to drink miso every day for lunch. The potent elixir is thought to help purify the blood, protecting it from the onslaught of vehicle exhaust fumes and keeping the officers healthy.

Miso is fermented soybean paste, but don't let the frumpy description fool you. This superfood's superpower is its fermentation process, which creates many health properties. It is rich in probiotics, which help maintain our microbiome kingdom.

Miso boosts digestion, aiding the immune system and helping fight disease. A healthy gut also reduces the risk of IBS and other inflammatory diseases. Miso contains many vitamins and minerals: B-complex, vitamin K, manganese, zinc, calcium, proteins, and the elusive plant-based vitamin B12 (B12 is typically found in animal sources). These nutrients support essential structures like the bones and nervous system. Miso can help balance the body's pH level, which can be beneficial for overall health. Miso is alkaline, which can help counteract the negative effects of acidic foods like coffee, alcohol, sweets, and meat. Some East Asians use miso to help with acid indigestion, hangovers, and upset stomachs. Miso can also help reduce symptoms of GERD, such as dyspepsia and reflux. Miso is rich in digestive enzymes and can protect the stomach lining. Miso's restorative nature may prevent inflammatory issues such as gastritis, gastric ulcers, or duodenal ulcers, and even gastric cancer. Miso may also lower cholesterol and improve mental health.

Miso is a staple in macrobiotic cooking. Macrobiotic cooking emphasizes whole, unrefined plant-based foods, with a balance of grains, vegetables, and beans, prepared with minimal processing for optimal health and harmony with nature.

Note: Miso can be high in sodium, so choose low-sodium varieties when restricting salt intake. See Specialty Ingredients (page 215).

(Continued)

Makes 4 servings

Ingredients:
4 tablespoons miso paste
4 cups vegetable stock, divided

Garnishes:
1 sheet nori
½ cup scallions, thinly sliced
¼ cup firm tofu, cubed

Directions:
Dissolve the miso in ¼ cup of the stock to make a smooth paste. Simmer the remaining stock on low heat. Whisk the miso paste into the stock. Slowly stir until fully combined. Ladle into deep bowls and add garnish if desired.

Roasted Garlic

Garlic is a superfood indicated in so many health benefits that it's difficult to choose a particular body system; however, the immune system stands out. Garlic contains a remarkable ingredient called allicin, formed when garlic is crushed or chopped (exposed to air). Allicin exhibits antiviral properties, potentially hindering the ability of viruses to multiply and spread within the body and reducing the severity and duration of illnesses like the common cold and flu. Allicin and other compounds in garlic may activate natural killer cells, which play a crucial role in the body's early defense against infections. This activation helps the immune system identify and eliminate foreign invaders more effectively. Oregano also offers potential benefits for the immune system thanks to its unique blend of compounds. Carvacrol and thymol, two main components, possess antimicrobial properties that may help fight off bacterial and potentially viral infections. Both garlic and oregano are rich in antioxidants, which combat free radicals that can damage cells and weaken the immune response. By neutralizing these harmful molecules, garlic helps maintain a strong immune system ready to fight off infections. Garlic has anti-inflammatory properties, which may reduce inflammation throughout the body.

(Continued)

Makes 4 servings

Ingredients:
3 whole bulbs (heads) garlic, peeled and roughly chopped
3 tablespoons butter or olive oil
1 onion, peeled and chopped
¼ cup apple cider vinegar or plain kombucha (see Specialty Ingredients, page 215)
1 tablespoon fresh oregano, chopped
3 cups stock
2 medium russet potatoes, scrubbed and cubed
½ cup cream or nondairy milk
Sea salt and freshly ground black pepper, to taste

Directions:
Preheat oven to 400°F. Remove the tips off the heads of the garlic bulbs and place the bulbs cut-side up in the center of a piece of aluminum foil. Sprinkle each head with olive oil and wrap the foil up around them, creating little garlic packets wrapped in foil. Place the garlic in a small baking dish and roast for 30 minutes, or until it is soft. Remove the bulbs from the oven. Open the packages so the garlic can cool.

Melt the butter in a heavy-bottomed saucepan over medium-high heat. Add the onion, stirring occasionally. Cook until the onion is translucent, about 5 minutes. Add vinegar, oregano, stock, and potatoes to the pot. Bring the pot to a simmer, reduce the heat, cover the pot, and continue to simmer for 30 to 45 minutes, or until the potatoes are soft.

When the garlic is cool enough to handle, squeeze the clove directly into the saucepan. When the soup has cooled, use an immersion blender (or blender) to partially puree the soup, so that is has some chunks remaining. Add cream and stir. Taste the soup and adjust seasoning with the sea salt and pepper. Serve warm.

Garnish suggestion: Soup Croutons (page 209), shredded Parmesan or nutritional yeast, drizzle of olive oil, and chopped chive or scallion. Also great with kimchi or other raw-fermented vegetable!

Kimchi Jjigae (Kimchi Stew)

Kimchi's immune-boosting potential comes from its lacto-fermentation process, which creates probiotics like lactobacillus. These probiotics play a crucial role in a healthy gut health microbiome, strengthening the immune system and producing chemicals needed for mental health (the gut-brain axis). A healthy gut microbiome is linked to a more robust immune response, as it can help train and regulate the cells to better identify and combat foreign invaders. Seaweed is a key superfood that helps with detoxification. Seaweed is a robust source of minerals like iodine, magnesium, and calcium, which are important for various bodily functions, including the thyroid. A healthy thyroid is vital for overall metabolism and toxin clearance. Seaweed contains specific compounds like alginate and fucoidan that can bind heavy metals and toxins, preventing their absorption into the bloodstream. These bound toxins are then naturally eliminated from the body through the digestive system. Seaweed contains antioxidants that can protect the liver, the body's primary detoxification organ. A healthy liver is crucial for efficient toxin removal. Seaweed's fiber content can aid digestion, ensuring regular bowel movements and efficient elimination of waste products, including toxins. Kimchi is also high in vitamin C, an essential nutrient for immune function, further supporting the body's defense against infections.

See Specialty Ingredients (page 215).

(Continued)

Makes 6 servings

Ingredients:
Optional: ½ pound ground pork
4 cups stock
1 tablespoon tamari
1 tablespoon honey
1 tablespoon white rice vinegar
1 (14-ounce) package extra-firm tofu, patted dry and cubed
1 cup fresh whole enoki (straw) or fresh shiitake mushrooms, thinly sliced
2 cups chopped raw kimchi, including its juice

Garnish:
2 stalks scallions, thinly sliced
2 sheets nori seaweed, cut into ½-inch strips (use scissors)

Optional:
Cooked basmati rice or healthy ramen noodles

Directions:
If using pork: brown the pork in a skillet and set aside.

Prepare all the ingredients in separate bowls and set aside. These will be used in assembling the soup.

Place the stock, tamari, honey, and vinegar in a pot, and bring to a simmer.

Assemble the soup: add a spoonful each of pork (if using), tofu, and mushrooms into each bowl. Add rice or ramen, if using. Add ½ cup of kimchi, including its juice. Ladle soup into each bowl. Garnish with scallions and nori.

Ginger Carrots with Crispy Chickpeas

Carrots offer a significant boost to the immune system, thanks to their rich content of vitamins and antioxidants. Vitamin A, converted from the abundant beta-carotene in carrots, plays a crucial role in maintaining healthy mucous membranes lining the respiratory, digestive, and urogenital tracts. Vitamin C in carrots helps white blood cells, which are vital for fighting off infections, function effectively. Carrots contain antioxidants that combat free radicals, harmful molecules that can damage immune cells and weaken the body's defense system. Carrots can be part of a healthy diet for people with diabetes, as the soluble fiber can help regulate blood sugar levels by slowing the movement of food through the digestive system. Glucose is absorbed more gradually, preventing sudden spikes in blood sugar levels. Soluble fiber can improve insulin sensitivity—how body cells respond to insulin. Healthy insulin sensitivity can prevent conditions like type 2 diabetes, heart disease, and obesity.

Makes 4 servings

Ingredients:
2 pounds carrots
2 onions
4 garlic cloves, peeled
4 tablespoons olive oil
½ cup tahini (see Specialty Ingredients, page 215)
2 tablespoons fresh ginger root, peeled and sliced
2 teaspoons turmeric
1 teaspoon paprika
1 teaspoon cumin
1 teaspoon black pepper
Sea salt, to taste
4 cups chicken stock, divided

(Continued)

GARNISH:
Fresh cilantro, chopped
Plain yogurt or kefir

Directions:
Peel carrots and cut into 2-inch lengths. Cut onions into quarters. Spread carrots, onions, and garlic on a baking sheet lined with parchment paper. Drizzle with olive oil. Roast the vegetables at 425°F for 40 minutes or until "fork tender." Remove one chunk of carrot, slice thinly, and set aside for garnish.

Place the roasted vegetables, tahini, ginger, spices, and 2 cups of stock into a blender and process until smooth but with some texture. Use the extra 2 cups of stock to add slowly to obtain the desired thickness. Garnish with cilantro and yogurt.

Crispy Chickpeas

Nutritional yeast is a rich source of nutrients, including B vitamins, zinc, and protein, which all contribute to a vibrant immune system.

Ingredients:
1 (14-ounce) can chickpeas, drained and patted dry
1 tablespoon olive oil
1 tablespoon nutritional yeast
1 teaspoon garlic powder
½ teaspoon sea salt

Directions:
Toss all ingredients together and spread on a lined baking sheet. Roast in the oven at 425°F for 40 minutes. Can be done ahead of time.

Kefir Mint

Ever tried kefir? It's time to get acquainted! Kefir has over thirty types of probiotic bacteria, versus a few in yogurt. Kefir's probiotics are "right turning bacteria," which means they are stronger than yogurt's "left turning bacteria" ("turning" refers to the organism's observed movement under the microscope). Kefir's probiotic bacteria are strong enough to make it past the stomach acids and actually establish whole colonies in the gastrointestinal tract, becoming the dominant bacteria. Kefir's colonies are strong enough that they can survive the onslaught of antibiotics! Furthermore, kefir's probiotics offer antibiotic properties without the side effects. Kefir can provide support with a wide range of digestive and respiratory ailments, such as acid reflux, constipation, lactose intolerance, IBS, and allergy and asthma symptoms. Kefir's antibiotic nature may reduce or eliminate cold and flu symptoms. Its array probiotics may promote deep sleep and a natural positive feeling. An additional benefit of kefir relates to heart health. Kefir contains bioactive peptides, small protein fragments with ACE-inhibiting properties. These peptides mimic the function of certain medications, potentially preventing the narrowing of blood vessels and reducing blood pressure. Finally, mint is known for its soothing effect on the digestive system. It contains compounds that can help relax the muscles of the digestive tract, reducing discomfort and promoting digestion. Mint can also help alleviate symptoms like indigestion, bloating, and nausea.

See Specialty Ingredients (page 215).

(Continued)

Makes 4 servings

Ingredients:
⅓ cup basmati rice, rinsed
5 cups chicken stock
1 egg, room temperature
1½ cups plain kefir, room temperature*
1 tablespoon tapioca flour
1 teaspoon salt (more if needed)
2 tablespoons unsalted butter
1 bunch fresh mint, finely chopped

Directions:
Place the rice and stock in a large pot and bring to a simmer. Cover and cook for about 40 minutes until the rice is fully cooked and has fallen apart. In a large bowl, beat the egg, and then whisk in kefir, flour, and salt until perfectly smooth.

Once the rice is cooked, turn the heat off. Using a ladle, slowly add about 1½ cups of the rice and stock, ½ cup at a time, to the kefir and egg mixture, stirring well after each addition. Do this slowly to prevent curdling of the kefir mixture. Add this mixture back into the pot. Reduce heat to low and gently simmer for a few minutes, stirring often. Meanwhile, in a small pan, add the butter and mint and sauté gently for a few minutes. Swirl the sautéed mint butter into the simmering soup. Serve warm.

---

*While kefir is preferred for the health benefits, yogurt may be substituted. Choose an organic whole-milk or Greek variety.

Thai Red Curry Noodle

Curry's immune-boosting potential comes from a powerhouse of ingredients. Turmeric, often a key component, contains curcumin, a powerful anti-inflammatory, which can reduce the body's response to harmful substances and promote healing. Curry spices like ginger and chili peppers contain antioxidants and compounds that further combat inflammation. This combined anti-inflammatory effect helps reduce stress on the immune system, allowing it to function more efficiently. These spices are rich in antioxidants like vitamins C and E, which neutralize free radicals that damage cells and contribute to chronic diseases. By protecting cells and reducing inflammation, curry's diverse blend of spices creates an environment where the immune system can function optimally. Think of this soup as one spicy delicious decongestant!

See Specialty Ingredients (page 215).

(Continued)

Makes 4 servings

Ingredients:
2 tablespoons high-heat vegetable oil, such as grapeseed or avocado
½ pound boneless, skinless chicken (breasts or thighs), cut into chunks
4 cloves garlic, peeled and minced
1 bell red pepper, diced
1 onion, peeled and diced
1 tablespoon Thai-style red curry paste
1 tablespoon tamari
1 tablespoon fresh ginger root, peeled and grated
1 teaspoon raw honey
3 cups chicken stock
1 cup coconut milk
1 package of gluten-free ramen noodles

Garnishes:
Green onion, thinly sliced
Fresh cilantro leaves, chopped
Fresh basil leaves, chopped
Lime wedges

Directions:
In a large heavy-bottomed saucepan, heat the oil and sauté the chicken for 2 minutes. Add the garlic, red pepper, and onion and sauté for another few minutes. Add the curry paste, tamari, ginger, and honey. Stir well, until the paste has completely dissolved. Add the stock and coconut milk. Gently simmer for 20 minutes, being careful to not let boil.

Before serving, add noodles and cook for 3 minutes. Garnish and enjoy immediately!

Parsley Soup with Mini Chicken Meatballs

Parsley is a versatile herb that offers numerous health benefits to the immune system. Packed with vitamins A, C, and K, and minerals iron and potassium, parsley acts as a powerful antioxidant. These nutrients help neutralize harmful free radicals, reducing oxidative stress and protecting cells from damage. Parsley contains flavonoids, compounds that have anti-inflammatory properties. This helps reduce inflammation throughout the body, including in the immune system, allowing it to function optimally and fight off infections more effectively. Oats are used in place of breadcrumbs to eliminate wheat, which can be detrimental to immune and gut health. Oats are a nutritious grain packed with fiber, vitamins, and minerals that support a strong immune system. The beta-glucans in oats help regulate gut health, which plays a crucial role in immune function, while the antioxidants help protect cells from damage and inflammation. Use gluten-free oats for gluten-sensitive diets (see Specialty Ingredients, page 215).

(Continued)

Makes 4 servings

Meatballs:
1 pound ground chicken or turkey
1 egg
1 cup quick oats
½ cup grated Parmesan
Sea salt and freshly ground black pepper, to taste

Directions:
Preheat oven to 400°F. Gently combine all the meatball ingredients (overworking this mixture may result in a rubbery texture). Use a fork or work by hand. Form into small balls, about 3 tablespoons in size. Roast on a baking sheet for 30 minutes. Set aside.

Soup:
2 bunches fresh parsley
1 bunch fresh mint leaves
2 tablespoons olive oil
1 onion, peeled and finely chopped
4 garlic cloves, finely chopped
1 teaspoon fresh lemon zest
2 tablespoons fresh-squeezed lemon juice
4 cups chicken stock
Sea salt and freshly ground pepper, to taste

Directions:
Prepare the herbs: dip the parsley leaf-side down into a large bowl of cold water. Immerse the whole bunch, including the stems. Swish it around gently, allowing the sand and dirt to fall to the bottom of the bowl. Lift out the parsley and shake off the excess water. Repeat this a few times, then pat dry the parsley and set aside. Wash and pat dry the mint.

Warm the olive oil in a heavy saucepan and sauté the onion and garlic for five minutes, stirring frequently until soft.

Just before serving: Chop the parsley and mint together finely, including the stems (for extra nutrition). This can be done in a food processor, but be careful to rough-chop the herbs (versus pureeing them). Add the chopped herbs to the sautéed vegetables along with the zest, lemon juice, and stock. Taste the stock and adjust seasoning with salt and pepper. Adjust the thickness with additional stock, if preferred. Ladle the soup into bowls. Add a few chicken meatballs, then garnish with a few grinds of cracked pepper.

Leftover meatballs can be frozen and used for pasta or other meal.

Nervous System

The nervous system controls and coordinates all of the body's functions, allowing us to interact with the world. It is made up of a complex network of cells and tissues all communicating with each other. The nervous system acts as the conductor in the body's orchestra, regulating all the other systems. It coordinates the movement of food through the digestive tract and the secretion of digestive enzymes, regulates the release of hormones in the endocrine system, monitors heart rate and blood pressure in the circulatory system, and controls the rate and depth of breathing in the respiratory system. The nervous system plays a crucial role in regulating the integumentary system, controlling blood flow to the skin, adjusting body temperature through sweating and shivering, and sending signals to muscles to contract for movement, protecting the skin from injury.

One of the primary ways the nervous system prevents disease is by controlling the body's stress response. When faced with stress, the nervous system releases hormones such as cortisol and adrenaline, which help the body to cope with challenging situations. However, chronic stress can lead to imbalances in these hormones, increasing the risk of various health problems, including heart disease, high blood pressure, and depression. The nervous system helps to regulate the stress response, preventing excessive stress and its associated health risks. The nervous system communicates with the immune system, regulating the production of immune cells and the release of immune molecules, helping it to effectively fight off infections and diseases.

The nervous system is responsible for thought, memory, and learning. It allows us to think, reason, and solve problems. It receives sensory information from the environment through the senses of sight, hearing, taste, smell, and touch. This information is then transmitted to the brain for processing. It controls movement by sending motor commands from the brain to the muscles. This allows us to move our bodies and perform tasks. The nervous system helps to maintain homeostasis, which is the body's ability to keep a stable internal environment. It does this by regulating functions such as heart rate, blood pressure, and body temperature.

It plays a crucial role in our emotions. It helps us to experience and express emotions such as joy, sadness, anger, and fear.

Turkey Dinner in a Bowl

Most of us in the United States are familiar with the Thanksgiving nap. Turkey contains high amounts of an amino acid called tryptophan, which helps to create serotonin. Serotonin produces feelings of calm contentment, helping us relax and sleep. Turkey is also a good source of minerals like magnesium and zinc, which support healthy nerve function and improve sleep. Zinc helps convert tryptophan into serotonin, which then turns into melatonin, the sleep hormone. Turkey also contains B vitamins—tiny helpers for our brain cells that improve the mind, both while we're awake and in our dreams.

Rosemary can act as an antioxidant, antimicrobial, and anti-inflammatory compound. In traditional folk medicine, Rosemary is known as a fever reducer and analgesic. Sage is a classic herb for colds and sore throats and also known as a fever reducer. Parsley is rich in flavonoids that may help improve mood and reduce anxiety. These compounds may help increase levels of neurotransmitters associated with well-being, such as serotonin and dopamine.

(Continued)

Makes 4 servings

Ingredients:
3 tablespoons olive oil
1 onion, peeled and chopped
2 large carrots, chopped
2 celery stalks, chopped
1 sweet potato, peeled and cubed
1 butternut (winter) squash, peeled and cubed
1 handful green beans, cleaned and cut in half (or 1 cup frozen)
6 cups chicken or turkey stock
2 cups cooked turkey meat chunks
1 tablespoon fresh sage, chopped
1 tablespoon fresh rosemary, chopped
Sea salt and black pepper, to taste

Garnish:
Fresh chopped parsley
Healthy cranberry sauce (see Specialty Ingredients, page 215)

Directions:
Heat the olive oil in a large pot over medium-high heat. Add the onion, carrots, and celery. Sauté for 10 minutes. Add the sweet potato, squash, and green beans, and sauté for a few minutes. Add poultry stock and turkey meat and bring to just a boil. Simmer soup for 15 minutes, or until the potato and squash are tender. Add sage and rosemary. Adjust seasoning with sea salt and black pepper.

Garnish with fresh parsley. Delicious served with Herby Biscuits (page 191) smeared with healthy cranberry sauce (see Specialty Ingredients, page 215)

Hunter's Stew

Venison and other game meats are strong nervous system supporters. Venison is packed with B vitamins, especially B12 and B6, helping brain cells communicate with each other, and supporting learning, memory, and improving mood. Venison contains iron, which helps carry oxygen to your brain, keeping it energized and focused. Eating venison can give the nervous system a boost of energy and well-being. Bacon, while high in saturated fat, does contain nutrients that can benefit the nervous system. It is a source of B vitamins, particularly B12, which is crucial for nerve function and can help prevent neurological conditions like anemia. If venison is unavailable, try game meat like bison or lamb. Otherwise, use grass-fed beef or heritage pork.

(Continued)

Makes 4 servings

Ingredients:
4 slices reduced-salt bacon, cut into small pieces
1 pound venison, cut into large chunks
1 onion, peeled and chopped
3 cloves garlic, peeled and chopped
1 large tomato, chopped
2 potatoes, cut into small cubes
1 teaspoon fresh rosemary leaves, chopped
1 tablespoon prepared horseradish
1 tablespoon Worcestershire sauce
1 cup dark beer or ginger brew
4 cups stock
2 bunches kale, cut into small pieces
Sea salt and black pepper, to taste

Directions:
In a large saucepan, fry the bacon over medium heat for 10 minutes. Add the venison and continue to cook until the meat is brown and the bacon is crispy.

Add onion and garlic and sauté for 5 minutes, then add the tomato and cook for another 5 minutes. Next, add the potatoes, rosemary, horseradish, Worcestershire sauce, and beer. Give the beer a moment to foam and then subside, gently stirring. Add the stock. Slowly bring to *just* a boil, then add kale, salt, and pepper. Reduce heat and simmer soup, partially covered, for 2 hours or until the meat is soft and tender.

Green Tea with Smoked Salmon

Green tea contains caffeine, a mild stimulant that enhances alertness and focus. It has about half the caffeine of coffee per serving, so its effects are less jolting and more sustaining. Green tea also contains L-theanine, an amino acid with calming properties. This unique combination creates a balanced effect on the nervous system, promoting both alertness and relaxation. L-theanine increases the activity of the inhibitory neurotransmitter GABA, which has calming effects, promoting a focused and clear mind. This can help reduce anxiety, stress, and feelings of overwhelm, promoting a sense of well-being. Green tea may improve cognitive function, memory, and reaction time. Green tea's antioxidants, like catechins, protect brain cells from damage caused by free radicals, potentially reducing the risk of neurodegenerative diseases like Alzheimer's and Parkinson's, and may reduce the risk of chronic diseases like heart disease, cancer, and cognitive decline.

Makes 2–3 servings

Ingredients:
1 cup cooked white or brown basmati rice
3 cups hot, strong green tea
Miso or tamari
1 bunch fresh parsley, chopped
1 tablespoon sesame seeds
4 ounces smoked salmon, cut into chunks
Freshly ground black pepper, to taste

Directions:
Prepare the mise en place: place each ingredient in a separate container, ready to assemble the soup. For assembly: divide the rice between two bowls. Divide and pour hot tea into each of the bowls. Add a spoonful of miso or tamari to each bowl and stir. Sprinkle parsley and sesame seeds on top, and then add smoked fish on top of each. Season with freshly ground black pepper.

Hangover Helper

There is a reason Bloody Marys are consumed at Sunday brunch; they have medicinal qualities that can aid Saturday hangovers. Garlic contains an amino acid called S-allyl cysteine, which helps neutralize acetaldehyde, a toxic by-product of alcohol metabolism. This can potentially reduce some hangover symptoms like nausea and fatigue. Horseradish contains allyl isothiocyanate, a compound that may stimulate blood circulation and potentially aid in the removal of toxins and metabolic waste products produced during alcohol breakdown. This can contribute to faster recovery and alleviate symptoms like nausea and sluggishness.

Both garlic and horseradish are a good source of antioxidants, which can help combat the free radical damage caused by alcohol consumption. This may contribute to faster recovery by reducing oxidative stress in the body.

Gentle suggestion: The best way to avoid a hangover is, of course, abstaining from alcohol! xo

Makes 2–3 servings

Ingredients:
1 whole bulb (head) garlic
2 tablespoons olive oil
2 cups healthy tomato juice (see Specialty Ingredients, page 215)
2 cups stock
2 tablespoons Worcestershire sauce
2 tablespoons horseradish, freshly grated, plus more for garnish
Tabasco, to taste

Directions:
Peel and thinly slice the garlic cloves. Sauté the garlic in olive oil over low heat for a few minutes. The garlic should soften but not brown. Add the remaining ingredients and simmer gently for 15 minutes.

Garnish with extra fresh horseradish and Tabasco.

Chocolate Love

It's no wonder we crave chocolate when feeling depressed and stressed. Chocolate offers several benefits to the nervous system. Flavonols improve cognitive function, potentially enhancing memory and reaction time and even protecting against age-related cognitive decline. Dark chocolate contains compounds like tryptophan and phenethylamine, which can stimulate the production of feel-good neurotransmitters like serotonin and dopamine, potentially improving mood and reducing stress.

Anandamide is a naturally occurring cannabinoid produced by the body that interacts with the endocannabinoid system, influencing mood, pain perception, appetite, and memory. Chocolate contains small amounts of anandamide, along with other chemicals that inhibit the breakdown of anandamide by the body, potentially enhancing its effects. This may contribute to the pleasurable feeling people get from eating chocolate. The cocoa in dark chocolate is rich in flavonols, powerful antioxidants that may lower blood pressure, reduce inflammation, and improve blood flow. This can potentially lower the risk of heart disease and stroke. Flavanols may improve insulin sensitivity, potentially aiding in blood sugar control and reducing the risk of type 2 diabetes.

(Continued)

Makes 2 servings

Ingredients:
1 tablespoon cornstarch
2 tablespoons water
1½ cups unsweetened almond milk
12 ounces bittersweet dark chocolate, roughly chopped
1 teaspoon pure vanilla extract
½ teaspoon chili powder
¼ teaspoon cinnamon
1 teaspoon orange zest

Garnish:
Grated chocolate
Dehydrated strawberries
Vanilla yogurt
Shredded coconut

Directions:
In a small bowl, mix the cornstarch and the water together to form a milky paste similar to the consistency of cream. Set aside.

In a medium saucepan, heat the almond milk to a simmer over medium heat.

Remove from heat, add the chocolate, and whisk well until the chocolate melts completely. Add the cornstarch paste, return to medium heat, and reheat, whisking continuously, for a few minutes, until the soup is thick and smooth.

Reduce the heat to very low, and simmer for a few minutes, stirring gently and consistently to thoroughly cook the cornstarch. Turn off the heat and whisk in the vanilla, chili powder, cinnamon, and orange zest. Divide the soup between two bowls and garnish. If too thick, add a splash of almond milk. Enjoy warm.

Maple Blueberry

Blueberries boast one of the highest antioxidant levels among fruits, including anthocyanins, which create the vibrant blue color. Anthocyanins help repair damaged proteins in the vein walls, improving overall vein strength and health. Its anti-inflammatory properties can help with conditions like varicose veins. Chronic inflammation can be a risk factor in cardiovascular issues. Anthocyanins help relax the inner muscles in blood vessels, which improves blood flow. Blueberry consumption may decrease arterial stiffness, which is a risk factor for cardiovascular disease. Blueberries contain nitric oxide, which helps widen blood vessels and can lower blood pressure. Blueberries may protect brain function and improve memory. Their antioxidants may benefit neurons and potentially slow down age-related cognitive decline. These antioxidants combat free radicals, harmful molecules linked to chronic diseases like heart disease, cancer, and cognitive decline. Blueberries can contribute to a healthy heart by lowering blood pressure and reducing "bad" LDL cholesterol levels. Blueberries are relatively low in sugar and high in fiber, which can help regulate blood sugar levels and improve insulin sensitivity, potentially reducing the risk of type 2 diabetes. The fiber content also aids in managing cholesterol and promoting overall cardiovascular health.

Veins are blue, so when you think of veins, think blueberries!

(Continued)

Makes 2 servings

Ingredients:
¼ cup water
½ cup pure maple syrup
½ cup orange juice or kombucha
Grated zest of 1 lemon
½ teaspoon cinnamon
12 ounces blueberries, fresh or defrosted
1 cup Greek yogurt

Garnish:
Whole blueberries
Thin slice of lemon
Sprinkle granola
White chocolate curls or gratings

Directions:
Heat the water in a small saucepan and bring *just* to a boil. Add maple syrup, stirring until it is dissolved. Let cool. Place all the ingredients into a blender and blend until smooth. Chill at least for 1 hour before serving. Divide into small bowls, garnish, and serve.

Circulatory System

The circulatory system, or cardiovascular system, is a complex network of blood vessels and the heart that transports blood throughout the body. The circulatory system prevents disease by ensuring adequate oxygen delivery to tissues. The heart is a pump, carrying oxygen-rich blood from the lungs to cells and tissues. Oxygen is essential for cellular respiration, the process by which cells convert nutrients into energy. Insufficient oxygen delivery can lead to tissue damage and various diseases, including heart and peripheral artery disease and stroke.

    The circulatory system plays a crucial role in nutrient delivery and waste removal. Blood carries nutrients such as glucose, amino acids, and vitamins from the digestive system to cells. Nutrients are essential for growth, repair, and energy production. The circulatory system removes waste products from cells, like carbon dioxide and urea, and transports the waste to the lungs and kidneys for elimination.

    The circulatory system regulates blood pressure. The heart pumps blood through the vessels, creating pressure that forces the blood to flow. Blood vessels help to regulate this pressure by adjusting their diameter. A healthy circulatory system ensures that blood vessels function properly. High blood pressure can damage blood vessels and increase the risk of heart disease, stroke, and kidney disease.

    The circulatory system affects immune function. Blood contains white blood cells, which are essential for fighting off infections. The circulatory system transports white blood cells to sites of infection, where they help to destroy pathogens. Additionally, the circulatory system helps to remove waste products from the body, which can help to prevent infections.

    The circulatory system also plays a role in regulating body temperature. Blood can help to distribute heat throughout the body, helping to maintain proper temperature. When the body is too hot, blood vessels dilate, allowing more blood to flow near the surface of the skin, where heat can be dissipated. When the body is too cold, the blood vessels constrict, reducing blood flow to the skin and conserving heat.

The circulatory system plays a crucial role in disease prevention by ensuring adequate oxygen delivery, nutrient delivery, waste removal, blood pressure regulation, immune function, and temperature regulation. By maintaining a healthy circulatory system, individuals can reduce their risk of a variety of diseases and improve their overall quality of life.

Triple Corn

Whole corn offers a surprising range of benefits for the heart and circulatory system. Its fiber content helps lower cholesterol by binding to it in the digestive tract and preventing absorption. Corn is rich in potassium, a mineral that helps regulate blood pressure by counteracting the effects of sodium. This reduces stress on the heart and circulatory system, lowering the risk of heart attack and stroke. Corn contains antioxidants like lutein and zeaxanthin, which protect cells from damage and potentially reduce inflammation, a factor contributing to heart disease. Corn provides vitamin B6, crucial for maintaining healthy homocysteine levels. High homocysteine levels are a risk factor for heart disease. Adequate B6 intake is essential for cardiovascular health.

Makes 4 servings

Ingredients:
6 ears fresh corn
4 cups stock
½ teaspoon salt
4 corn tortillas
¼ cup high-heat vegetable oil, such as grapeseed or avocado
2 tablespoons olive oil
2 shallot cloves, finely chopped
1 teaspoon turmeric
1 tablespoon lime juice
Slices of lime

Optional:
Sea salt and black pepper

(Continued)

Directions:
Remove the corn kernels from the cob. Set corn kernels aside.

Break each cob in half. Place the corncobs, stock, and salt in a large saucepan. Bring ingredients to a boil and then reduce to a simmer. Cook for 1 hour. Strain the stock mixture and compost the solids.

Prepare the garnish: Cut the tortillas into long thin strips about ¼ inch wide. Fry the strips on high heat in the ¼ cup of vegetable oil. Toss the strips with tongs quickly to prevent burning. (These crisp up quickly, so stay at the stove.) Set the cooked strips on a plate lined with paper towels and put aside.

Heat olive oil in the same saucepan used for the corncob broth. Add the chopped shallots and, while sautéing, season with turmeric. Adjust with salt and pepper, if desired.

Add 1 cup of the fresh corn and water into a blender and puree. (The naturally occurring cornstarch works as the soup's thickening agent.) Pour the pureed mixture back into the same saucepan with the shallots. Add the stock mixture and lime juice, stirring well. Bring the soup to a boil, reduce the heat, and gently simmer. Add the remaining corn kernels and continue cooking for 5 minutes.

Garnish soup with the crisped tortilla strips and a slice of lime.

Note: These crispy tortilla strips are a great garnish for soups, chili, or beans. This is a great way to utilize stale tortillas, so feel free to do a larger batch.

Beet Borscht

When you picture beets, they kind of resemble a heart. Beets are rich in nitrates, which help relax and widen blood vessels, potentially lowering blood pressure and improving blood flow throughout the body. This improved blood flow can enhance exercise performance by increasing oxygen uptake and reducing fatigue. Beets have long been considered an endurance or energy food, in this way. Their vibrant color comes from betalains, potent antioxidants that fight free radical damage throughout the body and protect against heart disease and even cancer. Beets are also a good source of essential vitamins and minerals like vitamin C for immunity, manganese and folate for thyroid health, and potassium for blood pressure regulation and are packed with fiber, promoting digestive health and potentially reducing the risk of diseases such as colon cancer. Beets are a versatile food, full of vitamins, minerals, antioxidants, fiber, and other plant compounds. You can't beat beets!

Serve hot or cold.

(Continued)

Makes 4 servings

Ingredients:
2 tablespoons olive oil
1 onion, peeled and thinly sliced
3 cloves garlic, thinly sliced
2 large beets, peeled and cubed
2 red potatoes, cubed
4 cups vegetable stock
3 tablespoons raw apple cider vinegar
1 teaspoon sea salt
1 teaspoon ground pepper

Garnishes:
Plain whole yogurt, kefir, or goat cheese
Fresh parsley, chopped

Directions:
In a large pot or Dutch oven, heat the olive oil on medium. Add the onion and cook for a few minutes, until it is soft and translucent. Add the garlic and cook for a few more minutes, stirring continuously to prevent the garlic from burning. (Add more olive oil, if necessary.) Add the beets and potatoes and stir well. Pour in just enough stock to cover the beet mixture (may be less than 4 cups).

Increase heat and bring the mixture to a boil, then reduce the heat to simmer for 45 minutes. Cook until the potatoes and beets are tender.

Cool the soup for a few minutes, and then blend until smooth. Add the remaining stock to thin the soup. Add the vinegar, salt, and pepper, to taste.

Garnish with plain yogurt, kefir, or goat cheese and chopped parsley.

White Bean and Pesto

Beans are a great source of both soluble and insoluble fiber. Soluble fiber helps to regulate blood sugar levels and lower LDL cholesterol, promoting smoother blood flow and potentially decreasing the risk of heart disease, stroke, and plaque buildup in arteries. Insoluble fiber helps to promote regularity and prevent constipation. Both types of fiber are essential for a healthy digestive system. White beans are a good source of potassium, a mineral that helps regulate blood pressure. Potassium balances sodium, promoting healthy blood pressure levels and reducing strain on the heart and circulatory system. White beans are high in copper, a component of several enzymes involved in the production of connective tissue, which provides structural support for blood vessels. Copper is essential for the absorption of iron, a mineral crucial for red blood cell production. Olive oil is a rich source of healthy monounsaturated fats that help lower LDL cholesterol while raising HDL ("good") cholesterol, further contributing to a healthy cardiovascular profile. Garlic contains allicin, flavonoids, and organosulfur (containing sulfur) compounds, which may help in reducing blood pressure, preventing blood clots, and reducing LDL levels. Both basil and garlic contain antioxidants that combat free radical damage. This helps protect blood vessels from damage and inflammation, potentially reducing the risk of atherosclerosis and other cardiovascular complications.

(Continued)

Makes 4 servings

Ingredients:
PESTO:
1 cup fresh basil leaves, packed
½ cup pine nuts or walnuts
¼ cup Parmesan cheese, grated
¼ cup extra-virgin olive oil
4 garlic cloves, minced
Sea salt and freshly ground pepper, to taste

SOUP:
3 tablespoons olive oil
1 onion, diced
4 garlic cloves, peeled and thinly sliced
2 (15-ounce) cans cannellini or white beans, drained and rinsed
4 cups stock
1 tablespoon fresh lemon zest
1 teaspoon red pepper flakes
Sea salt and freshly ground black pepper, to taste
4 large kale leaves, washed, de-stemmed, and cut into long thin strips

SUGGESTED GARNISH:
Soup Croutons (page 209)
Parmesan cheese
Drizzle olive oil

Directions:
Prepare the pesto: Place all ingredients into a blender. Pulse a few times, until the texture is mostly smooth. Set aside.

Prepare the soup: In a large saucepan, heat the olive oil on medium heat. Add the onion and garlic and sauté for a few minutes. Add the beans, stock, lemon zest, and pepper flakes. Season with salt and pepper, to taste.

Before serving, stir in the kale and pesto, and simmer for 10 minutes.

Roasted Lemon

Lemons are a rich source of vitamin C, an antioxidant that fights free radicals, potentially reducing the risk of chronic diseases like heart disease and certain cancers. Tahini (sesame nut paste) is a good source of monounsaturated and polyunsaturated fats, which can help lower LDL ("bad") cholesterol levels and increase HDL ("good") cholesterol levels. Coconut oil is high in MCTs (medium-chain triglycerides), a type of fat that is more easily digested and absorbed by the body compared to long-chain triglycerides (LCTs) found in most dietary fats. Together, tahini and coconut may help improve cholesterol levels, potentially reducing the risk of heart disease. MCT oil can also promote a feeling of fullness, which may lead to reduced calorie intake and weight loss. This, in turn, can positively impact heart health. Tahini contains lignans, which have antioxidant and anti-inflammatory properties that may positively impact cholesterol levels and reduce stress. Tahini consumption may help lower blood pressure and improve the functioning of the endothelium—the inner lining of the blood vessels. Lemons are also a good source of potassium, a mineral that helps regulate blood pressure and contributes to overall cardiovascular health. Additionally, the citric acid in lemons may help prevent kidney stones and contribute to a healthy urinary tract.

See Specialty Ingredients (page 215).

(Continued)

Makes 4 servings

Ingredients:
3 whole lemons
2 tablespoons coconut oil
1 onion, peeled and chopped
1 carrot, chopped
4 garlic cloves, peeled and chopped
½ cup uncooked brown rice
6 cups vegetable stock
2 tablespoons tahini
2 tablespoons miso paste
Juice of 1 lemon

Garnish:
1 bunch parsley, chopped
Freshly ground black pepper

Directions:
Roast the lemons: Preheat oven to 350°F. Remove both nubby ends of the lemons. Cut the lemons in half and slice thinly. Line a cookie sheet and place lemons over the sheet in one layer. Roast the lemons for 30 minutes. After roasting, roughly chop the lemon slices and set aside.

Warm the coconut oil in a large soup pot. Sauté the onion, carrot, and garlic for 10 minutes. Add the chopped lemon and rice, stirring well. Add most of the vegetable stock, reserving ½ cup of stock on the side. Bring the pot to a boil and then reduce to a simmer for about 30 minutes. While the soup is cooking, place the tahini, miso, lemon juice, and the remaining ½ cup of stock into a bowl, and whisk the ingredients until smooth. When the soup is done cooking, pour the tahini mixture slowly into the soup and mix well. To serve, sprinkle chopped parsley and freshly ground black pepper on top of each bowl.

Mushroom Barley

Mushrooms are a rich source of antioxidants, including beta-glucans. These can help protect cells from damage caused by free radicals, which are linked to heart disease. Beta-glucans may also lower cholesterol levels by binding to cholesterol in the digestive tract. Barley provides a great source of soluble fiber, which helps regulate cholesterol levels. Mushrooms contain various antioxidants, including selenium, vitamin C, and polyphenols, which can help protect cells from damage caused by free radicals. Mushrooms and barley contain various phytochemicals, such as lectins and ergosterol, which aid in reducing inflammation, improving blood vessel function, and regulating blood pressure. Ergosterol can be converted to vitamin D in the body, which plays a role in heart health. Mushrooms are a good source of potassium, essential for maintaining healthy blood pressure. The combination of antioxidants, fiber, and phytochemicals in mushroom barley soup offers a comprehensive approach to supporting cardiovascular health.

(Continued)

Makes 4 servings

Ingredients:
¼ cup olive oil, divided
8 ounces baby bella (crimini) mushrooms, dry-wiped clean and sliced
1 large onion, peeled and chopped
2 celery stalks, chopped
1 large carrot, chopped
4 garlic cloves, peeled and chopped
8 ounces fresh shiitake or white mushrooms, dry-wiped clean and sliced
½ cup canned organic crushed tomatoes
2 teaspoons cumin
1 teaspoon paprika
Tamari, to taste
Black pepper, to taste
4 cups stock
½ cup pearl barley, rinsed*
½ cup water
2 bunches fresh parsley, chopped

Directions:
Place a large heavy-bottomed saucepan over medium-high heat. Add half the olive oil and the baby bella mushrooms. Sauté the mushrooms for 5 minutes, until they begin to brown. Remove from the pot and set aside.

In the same pot, add the remaining olive oil to a medium-high heat. Then add onion, celery, carrot, garlic, and shiitake mushroom, and sauté for 5 minutes. Add tomatoes, cumin, paprika, tamari, and pepper. Cook for a few minutes, stirring continuously. Add stock, barley, and water. Bring to a boil, and then reduce heat to a simmer. Cook for about 45 to 60 minutes, until the barley is puffed and soft. Add the cooked sliced mushrooms back into the soup. Before serving, garnish generously with parsley.

---

* Or substitute with a gluten-free option, such as rice, millet, or buckwheat.

Sunshine Squash

Squash is packed with essential vitamins and minerals, including potassium, vitamin C, and beta-carotene, powerful antioxidants that protect cells from damage and reduce the risk of chronic diseases like cancer and heart disease. It is rich in potassium, which helps regulate blood pressure. Cayenne pepper contains capsaicin, a compound that can help lower blood pressure by dilating blood vessels. Capsaicin may aid in weight management, a crucial factor in heart health. Garlic, rich in allicin, may help reduce LDL ("bad") cholesterol and increase HDL ("good") cholesterol levels. Squash is a good source of dietary fiber, which also helps regulate cholesterol levels. Squash is both filling and low in calories, aiding in weight management. Cayenne and garlic contain antioxidants, which can help reduce the damage caused by free radicals and so help decrease the risk of heart disease. Furthermore, squash offers various B vitamins and minerals like magnesium, which are essential for energy production, nerve function, and overall well-being. All the herbs, plus the pumpkin seeds (containing zinc) help to boost the immune system.

(Continued)

Makes 4–6 servings

Ingredients:
3 tablespoons olive oil
1 onion, chopped
1 celery stalk, thinly sliced
1 carrot, thinly sliced
1 potato, peeled and diced
2 cloves garlic, peeled and sliced
1 tomato, chopped
1 tablespoon fresh ginger, peeled and grated
½ teaspoon turmeric
1 teaspoon curry powder
1 teaspoon cumin
½ teaspoon cayenne
Sea salt and black pepper, to taste
3 cups butternut squash, peeled and diced
4 cups vegetable stock

Garnish:
Sliced chives
Chopped fresh cilantro
Toasted pumpkin seeds
Plain yogurt

Directions:
In a large saucepan, heat olive oil on medium-high. Sauté the onion for a few minutes. Add celery, carrot, potato, and garlic, and continue to cook for another few minutes. Add tomato, ginger, turmeric, curry, cumin, cayenne, and salt and cook for another few minutes. This "blooms" the spices and brings out their best flavor. Next, add the squash and stock. Bring the soup to a boil and reduce the heat to simmer about 30 minutes, until the vegetables are very soft. Puree the soup in batches. This can be done with a blender, food processor, or immersion blender. Be careful pureeing the hot liquid, as it tends to "spit" and can burn. Serve hot with the suggested garnishes.

Chicken and Mushroom with Buckwheat Dumplings

Chicken, mushrooms, and parsley are a nutrient-packed trio that can significantly contribute to circulatory health. Chicken is a lean protein source that provides essential amino acids needed for building and repairing cardiovascular tissues. It is also rich in B vitamins, particularly niacin and vitamin B6, which help maintain healthy red blood cells and support heart function. Mushrooms are packed with antioxidants, including beta-glucans and ergothioneine, that help protect cells from damage caused by free radicals, which can contribute to atherosclerosis and other circulatory problems. They are also a good source of potassium, a mineral essential for regulating blood pressure. Parsley, a versatile herb, adds a flavorful boost to dishes while providing a range of health benefits. It is high in vitamin C, an antioxidant that helps strengthen blood vessels and protect against oxidative stress. Parsley also contains flavonoids, compounds that reduce inflammation and improve blood flow. Incorporating these three ingredients into one soup creates a delicious and nutritious meal that supports circulatory health and may reduce the risk of developing heart disease and other cardiovascular conditions.

(Continued)

Makes 4–6 servings

Buckwheat Dumplings

Buckwheat offers a significant benefit for individuals following a low-FODMAP diet. FODMAPs are short-chain carbohydrates that can be poorly absorbed by the small intestine, leading to digestive symptoms. Unlike many grains, buckwheat is naturally low in FODMAPs. This means it's less likely to trigger digestive symptoms like bloating, gas, and abdominal pain commonly experienced by those with FODMAP sensitivity. Furthermore, buckwheat isn't a grain, despite its confusing name. Buckwheat is a plant more related to rhubarb than grains. It's a good source of protein, fiber, and essential nutrients like magnesium and manganese. Unlike wheat, buckwheat is naturally gluten-free, making it a popular choice for people with celiac disease or gluten sensitivity. Additionally, buckwheat's high fiber content, primarily insoluble fiber, aids in digestive regularity and promotes a healthy gut environment, further contributing to digestive comfort.

See Specialty Ingredients (page 215).

Ingredients:
1 cup buckwheat flour
½ cup tapioca flour
1 tablespoon baking powder
1 teaspoon salt
¼ teaspoon pepper
1 cup milk
1 egg
3 tablespoons vegetable oil or ghee

Directions:
Sift together buckwheat flour, tapioca flour, baking powder, salt, and pepper.

In a separate bigger bowl, combine milk, egg, and oil. Mix well. Add the dry ingredients; stir until all ingredients are just combined. Dough should be wet. Let dough sit, covered, for 30 minutes, while you prepare the soup. Once soup has been simmering for about 10 minutes, generously wet hands and form dumplings into balls the size of golf balls. Gently place them into simmering soup. Cover pot and cook for 20 minutes.

Chicken and Mushroom Soup

Ingredients:
1 pound mushrooms, preferably crimini (portabella)
3 tablespoons butter or olive oil
1 pound boneless chicken breasts or thighs, cut into 1-inch chunks.
1½ teaspoons sea salt, divided
½ cup water
1 tablespoon high-heat vegetable oil, such as grapeseed or avocado
3 shallot cloves, peeled and chopped
3 garlic cloves, peeled and chopped
1 tablespoon fresh lemon juice
5 cups chicken stock
Buckwheat Dumplings (page 90)
1 bunch fresh parsley, chopped

Directions:
With a dry cloth, wipe all the dirt off the mushrooms. Remove the woody bottoms of the mushroom stems (save these trimmings and use for stock). Melt the butter in a frying pan over medium heat. Sauté the mushrooms for 5 minutes. Remove the mushrooms from the pan and set aside.

Add the chicken to the pan and sprinkle with ½ teaspoon of the salt. Cook over high heat for about 10 minutes, until the chicken starts to sear (brown) on both sides. Turn off the heat, remove the chicken from the pan, and set aside. (The chicken will finish cooking later.)

Turn the frying pan back on. When it is hot, add the ½ cup of water to deglaze the pan (releasing the sticky flavor adhered to the pan). With a wooden spoon, scrape up all the brown bits until they are all loosened up and mixed into the water.

In a large soup pot, heat the vegetable oil on medium heat. Sauté the shallots and garlic for a few minutes. Add the partially cooked chicken, the remaining teaspoon of salt, lemon juice, stock, and deglazed chicken stock from the frying pan. Bring slowly to a boil, then reduce the heat and simmer. After soup has been simmering for 10 minutes, add dumplings, cover pot, and simmer for an additional 20 minutes.

To serve, ladle the soup into bowls, then place the dumplings gently on top and sprinkle generously with chopped parsley.

Digestive System

The digestive system plays a crucial role in disease prevention. It functions as a physical barrier, immune defense, and regulator of the gut microbiome to help protect the body from a variety of digestive and systemic diseases.

The primary function of the digestive system is to absorb nutrients from food. These nutrients, including carbohydrates, proteins, fats, vitamins, and minerals, provide the body with energy, build and repair tissues, and support various metabolic processes. A healthy digestive system is crucial for preventing malnutrition and obesity. Malabsorption of nutrients can lead to deficiencies, while excessive absorption can contribute to weight gain. One of the primary ways the digestive system prevents disease is by acting as a physical barrier. The lining of the digestive tract, the mucosa, is composed of multiple layers that protect the underlying tissues from damage by harmful substances. The mucosa also contains mucus-producing cells that secrete a protective layer of mucus, which helps to trap and eliminate harmful bacteria and toxins.

Beyond its physical barrier function, the digestive system also plays a vital role in immune defense. The digestive system is home to a vast population of microorganisms known as the gut microbiome. This microbiome is home to a network of immune cells, including macrophages, neutrophils, and lymphocytes, which help to regulate the immune response and protect against pathogens. Disruptions in the gut microbiome have been linked to inflammatory bowel diseases (IBD) like Crohn's disease and ulcerative colitis. These conditions can lead to chronic inflammation, pain, and digestive problems. The digestive system eliminates waste products from the body, including toxins and undigested material, through stool. Irregular bowel movements can lead to constipation or diarrhea, both of which can impact overall health and comfort. Some hormones involved in digestion, such as ghrelin and leptin, also play a role in regulating appetite and energy expenditure. One exciting function of the digestive system is its ability to communicate with the brain through a neurological highway called the gut-brain axis. This connection influences mood, appetite, and stress response.

Digestive problems can significantly affect quality of life. Issues like bloating, gas, and abdominal pain can be distressing and interfere with daily activities. By ensuring efficient digestion and absorption of nutrients, the digestive system helps to prevent nutrient deficiencies, which can lead to a variety of health problems. A healthy digestive system is associated with a lower risk of chronic diseases, including heart disease, diabetes, and certain types of cancer.

Pumpkin Chili

Beans contain the amino acid (protein) glutamine, a major source of energy for the cells in the lining of the intestine. Glutamine also helps to keep the gut barrier strong and healthy, which is important for preventing leaky gut syndrome and other digestive disorders. Cinnamon and ginger aid digestion by stimulating the production of digestive enzymes and bile. Cayenne contains capsaicin, the compound responsible for the heat in chili peppers, which also plays a positive role in gut health by increasing the growth of beneficial gut bacteria and reducing inflammation. Capsaicin is used for pain relief and can help with ulcers.

Pumpkin and beans are rich sources of fiber, both insoluble and soluble. Insoluble fiber promotes smooth movement of food and waste through the gut. Soluble fiber helps lower cholesterol levels, manage blood sugar, and promote digestive health. By forming a gelatinous substance in the digestive tract, soluble fiber slows down the absorption of glucose, preventing spikes in blood sugar. This can be particularly beneficial for individuals with diabetes or prediabetes. Additionally, soluble fiber binds to cholesterol in the gut, helping to reduce its absorption and lower LDL ("bad") cholesterol levels. This can decrease the risk of heart disease.

(Continued)

Makes 6 servings

Ingredients:

2 tablespoons high-heat vegetable oil, such as grapeseed or avocado
1 onion, diced
4 cloves garlic, peeled and minced
1 red pepper, diced
1 pound ground beef or turkey
1 (15-ounce) can pumpkin puree or two cups fresh cooked pumpkin
1 (15-ounce) can black beans, drained and rinsed
1 (15-ounce) can tomatoes, drained and rinsed
1 tablespoon cocoa powder
1 tablespoon chili powder
1 teaspoon cumin
1 teaspoon cinnamon
½ teaspoon smoked paprika
¼ teaspoon cayenne
1 teaspoon sea salt
1 teaspoon black pepper
4 cups stock

Garnish:

Jalapeño, thinly sliced
Chopped cilantro or grated red onion
Cheese, sour cream or plain yogurt

Directions:

Heat oil in a large saucepan (or Dutch oven) on medium. Sauté onion, garlic, and pepper for a few minutes, until slightly soft. Add the ground turkey, chopping it with the spoon, and cook for a few minutes. Reduce heat to medium-low and stir in the pumpkin, beans, and diced tomatoes. Sprinkle the cocoa and spices on top of the chili mixture and stir well. Pour in stock and simmer for 60 minutes over low heat, stirring every now and then. Garnish as desired.

Spanish Lentil

Lentils are packed with fiber that promotes smooth digestion, satiates the appetite (feelings of fullness), and helps regulate the gut. Green olives are a great source of antioxidants, Vitamin E, and Vitamin K. They are also a rich source of healthy fats and contribute to gut health by potentially aiding in the absorption of nutrients and reducing inflammation. This soup's broth provides hydration and soothes irritation, while spices like garlic and oregano help stimulate digestive enzyme production. Tomatoes add another layer of fiber, plus are great sources of lycopene, an antioxidant that neutralizes free radicals—unstable molecules that can damage cells and contribute to various chronic diseases. Antioxidants may help reduce the risk of certain cancers, heart disease, and other conditions. Lycopene may improve heart health by lowering bad cholesterol (LDL) levels and increasing good cholesterol (HDL) levels. It may also help maintain healthy blood pressure. Lentils are rich in soluble fiber, a gelatinous substance that helps the digestive system run efficiently and also provides food for the probiotic (good) gut bacteria.

(Continued)

Makes 6 servings

Ingredients:
4 tablespoons olive oil
1 onion, peeled and chopped
2 carrots, diced
2 stalks celery, diced
4 cloves garlic, peeled and chopped
1 tablespoon fresh thyme, chopped
1 teaspoon smoked paprika
1 teaspoon sea salt
1 teaspoon black pepper
1 cup lentils
6 cups stock
1 (14-ounce) can diced tomatoes or two cups fresh ripe tomatoes, chopped
1 (5-ounce) bag fresh spinach, washed, dried, and roughly chopped
1 cup green olives, sliced in half

Optional:
½ cup cream, room temperature

Directions:
Heat the oil in a large pot over medium-high heat. Sauté the onion for 5 minutes. Add the carrots, celery, and garlic and cook for 5 more minutes. Mix in the thyme, smoked paprika, salt, and pepper and stir well. Add the lentils, stock, and tomatoes. Bring to a boil, and then reduce the heat to a simmer. Cover the pot and simmer for 45 minutes or until the lentils are soft. Just before serving, add the chopped spinach and olives, stirring until the spinach wilts. Add cream if desired.

Rice Congee

Congee, traditional rice porridge, boasts several health benefits. Its long, slow cooking process transforms rice into a soft, easily digestible meal, making it ideal for those with sensitive stomachs or recovering from illness. White basmati rice is easily digestible and gentle on the stomach. This gentle nature aids digestion by soothing inflammation and promoting nutrient absorption. Basmati rice is a good source of vitamins, minerals, and antioxidants, potentially boosting the immune system and overall well-being. Ginger contains compounds that can help relax the muscles in the digestive tract, reducing nausea and vomiting. Additionally, ginger can help stimulate the production of digestive enzymes, aiding in digestion and reducing bloating. Coconut oil can also aid digestion by acting as a prebiotic, supporting healthy gut bacteria. Coconut oil might help boost metabolism due to its medium-chain triglycerides (MCTs). These MCTs are absorbed and metabolized more quickly than long-chain triglycerides found in other oils. Additionally, coconut oil has antimicrobial properties, potentially fighting off harmful bacteria and viruses. Congee's high water content helps to keep the body hydrated, further supporting digestive health and potentially alleviating constipation. Congee's warm and comforting nature makes it a nourishing and versatile dish, suitable for breakfast, a light meal, or even a soothing remedy during recovery. Congee is a helpful meal for those suffering from nausea, IBS, or cancer or who are pregnant or recovering from surgery.

(Continued)

Makes 4 servings

Ingredients:
½ cup coconut oil
3 large shallot bulbs, peeled and sliced (about ½ cup)
Sea salt
¾ cup white basmati rice, rinsed and drained
2-inch piece ginger root, peeled, and cut into 4 slices
4–5 cups chicken stock
8 ounces cooked chicken breast, torn into bite-size pieces
2 tablespoons tamari or miso

Garnish:
Chili crisp sauce (see Specialty Ingredients, page 215)

Directions:
Prepare the crispy shallots: Line a cutting board or plate with several layers of paper towels. Place oil and shallots in a small saucepan and turn on high. It's important that shallots start in cold oil. When the oil starts to bubble, stir the shallots frequently for several minutes, until they darken. Scoop them out and put on paper towels to drain. Sprinkle shallots with sea salt.

Prepare Congee: Combine rice, ginger slices, and 4 cups of stock in a small saucepan. Bring to a boil and then reduce to the lowest heat setting. Simmer slowly for 3 hours, stirring occasionally to prevent sticking on the bottom.

Remove from heat. Congee will thicken up as it sits, so feel free to add more stock to achieve desired texture.

Remove ginger chunks. Add cooked chicken and tamari and stir gently.

Garnish with crispy shallots and chili crisp sauce.

Green Papaya

Green (unripe) papaya is a rich source of the digestive enzyme papain, which can aid in protein breakdown and potentially alleviate digestive issues like bloating and constipation. Papaya enzyme tablets are common digestive aids. Green papaya is also loaded with vitamin C. Vitamin C may play a role in promoting a healthy gut microbiome, which can contribute to better digestion and nutrient absorption. Vitamin C is necessary for the production of collagen, a protein that helps maintain the integrity of the lining of the digestive tract. Vitamin C is also known for its immune-boosting properties. A strong immune system can help fight off infections that can disrupt digestion, such as foodborne illness. Papaya's high fiber content promotes gut health and regularity, and its anti-inflammatory properties may benefit conditions like arthritis and asthma. Papaya seeds contain enzymes like papain, which can aid digestion by breaking down proteins. They can also help with bowel regularity and constipation due to their high fiber content. Papaya seeds have antioxidants and other compounds that may reduce inflammation in the body and have properties that could help eliminate intestinal parasites. The capsaicin in cayenne pepper has been shown to have anti-inflammatory properties and can potentially stimulate the production of mucus in the stomach, which can help protect and heal the stomach lining.

(Continued)

Makes 4–6 servings

Ingredients:
1 tablespoon olive oil
1 onion, peeled and finely chopped
2 cloves of garlic, peeled and minced
1-inch piece fresh ginger root, peeled and grated
1 medium-sized green papaya, peeled, deseeded*, and cubed
6 cups vegetable stock
1 teaspoon cayenne pepper or papaya seed pepper,* optional
Sea salt and pepper, to taste

Garnish:
1 bunch chopped fresh cilantro or sliced scallions

Directions:
In a large pot, heat the oil over medium heat. Add the onion, garlic, and ginger, and sauté a few minutes, until the onion is translucent. Add the green papaya cubes to the pot. Stir to combine. Pour in the stock and bring the mixture to a boil. Reduce the heat and simmer 20 minutes or until the papaya is tender. Add cayenne pepper or papaya seed pepper for added heat. Adjust seasoning with salt and pepper.

Garnish with cilantro or scallions (or both!).

*Papaya Seed Pepper

Rinse papaya seeds thoroughly to remove any remaining pulp.

Preheat oven to its lowest setting (around 200°F). Spread the seeds on a baking sheet lined with parchment paper and dry for 1 to 2 hours, checking and flipping them occasionally. They're done when they crumble easily. Once completely dry, grind the papaya seeds in a spice grinder or mortar and pestle for a peppery seasoning.

Note: Papaya seeds may interfere with fertility and are unsafe for pregnant women!

Lacto-Fermented Sauerkraut Stew

Live or *lacto-fermented* sauerkraut creates a wealth of probiotic bacteria, which contribute to a healthy gut microbiome by promoting digestive regularity and potentially reducing symptoms of digestive issues like IBS, Crohn's, and colitis. They are also great sources of fiber, aiding in digestive regularity.

Both parsnips and sauerkraut are great sources of vitamin C, an antioxidant that boosts the immune system, and vitamin K2, which plays a role in bone health and blood clotting. Parsnips offer significant amounts of potassium, a mineral that helps regulate blood pressure and contributes to heart health. The presence of polyacetylenes, compounds with potential anticancer properties, adds another layer of potential health benefits. Turkey is a good source of tryptophan, an amino acid that plays a role in the production of serotonin. Serotonin is a neurotransmitter that helps regulate mood, sleep, and appetite. Turkey bacon typically contains less saturated fat than regular bacon, which can help reduce cholesterol levels and lower the risk of heart disease. It tends to have lower sodium content compared to regular bacon, making it a better choice for individuals who are monitoring their sodium intake. Turkey bacon is also a leaner source of protein, providing essential nutrients without the excess fat and calories.

Note: Add sauerkraut into bowl just before serving, to retain its probiotic benefits.

(Continued)

Makes 4 servings

Ingredients:
8 ounces turkey bacon, chopped
1 onion, peeled and chopped
1 carrot, peeled and thinly sliced
1 parsnip, diced
2 potatoes, peeled and cubed
1 tablespoon fresh dill, chopped
1 teaspoon allspice
1 teaspoon black pepper
4 cups stock
2 cups raw lacto-fermented sauerkraut and its juice

Garnish:
Turkey bacon and sour cream

Directions:
Cook the chopped bacon over medium heat, stirring frequently to keep from burning. (Add a bit of water if it begins to stick.) When the bacon is crispy, remove 2 tablespoons and set aside for garnish. Add the onion, carrot, and parsnip. Continue to cook for another 5 minutes, stirring often. Add the potatoes, dill, allspice, and black pepper. Combine well. Add the stock, bring just to a boil, reduce heat, and simmer for 45 minutes.

Before serving, add sauerkraut and its juice into a bowl. Ladle soup over kraut. Garnish with the saved bacon pieces and a dollop of sour cream.

Green Matzo Ball

Beneficial herbs parsley, chives, dill, and arugula work synergistically for vibrant digestive health. Parsley is rich in volatile oils and flavonoids, which can help stimulate digestive enzymes. It also contains vitamin C, which aids in iron absorption. Chives are a good source of prebiotics, which can promote the growth of beneficial gut bacteria. These bacteria help break down food and absorb nutrients more efficiently. Dill contains compounds that can help relax the smooth muscles of the digestive tract, reducing bloating and gas. It also contains fiber, which can aid in digestion and prevent constipation. Arugula is also a good source of fiber and antioxidants. The fiber can help regulate bowel movements, while the antioxidants can help protect the digestive lining from damage. Spinach, another good source of fiber, also contains vitamins A, C, and K, as well as iron and magnesium, all of which are important for digestive health. While oxalates can sometimes interfere with mineral absorption, spinach also contains magnesium, which can help balance this effect. Spinach is rich in antioxidants like lutein and zeaxanthin, which can help protect the digestive lining from damage. Parsley is a natural diuretic. It helps eliminate waste products through the urinary system, contributing to clearer skin by reducing the burden on the body's detoxification processes. Parsley is also rich in vitamin K, crucial for healthy blood clotting and preventing bruises. To further support the digestive system, the matzo balls are made with gluten-free matzo meal.

(Continued)

Makes 4 servings

Ingredients:

MATZO BALLS:
3 eggs
½ cup vegetable stock
1 cup gluten-free matzo meal (see Specialty Ingredients, page 215)
¼ cup fresh parsley, finely chopped
2 tablespoons fresh chives, finely chopped
2 tablespoons fresh dill, finely chopped
2 tablespoons olive oil
½ teaspoon baking powder
½ teaspoon lemon zest
Sea salt and black pepper, to taste

SOUP:
4 tablespoons butter
1 onion, peeled and chopped
2 cloves garlic, peeled and chopped
4 cups vegetable stock
Juice of ½ a lemon
1 potato, peeled and diced
1 packed cup fresh spinach, chopped
1 packed cup arugula, chopped
1 bunch parsley, chopped
Sea salt and black pepper, to taste

Directions:

Prepare the matzo balls: In a large bowl, beat eggs well. Add the remaining ingredients and stir well. Cover and let sit for at least 2 hours on the counter or overnight in the refrigerator.

Prepare the soup. Melt butter in a large, heavy-bottomed saucepan. Sauté the onion and garlic for 5 minutes, stirring frequently. Add the stock, lemon juice, and potato. Simmer about 15 minutes, until the potato is soft. Add

(Continued)

spinach, arugula, and parsley, and cook for one more minute. Puree the hot soup carefully to avoid the blender "spitting." The broth will be very smooth, bright green, and beautiful. Return broth to saucepan and reheat for serving. Adjust taste with salt and pepper.

Cooking the matzo balls: Boil salted water in a pot. While water is heating, form the matzo dough into balls the size of large walnuts or golf balls. Gently place all the balls into the boiling salted water and simmer. Stir gently and occasionally for about 15 minutes, until the matzo balls are floating, puffed, and thoroughly cooked—pull one from the water at 15 minutes and cut it in half to check. The texture should be uniform in color and texture and lighter in color than its raw state. It should look fluffy, not dense. Using a slotted spoon, transfer the matzo balls into soup bowls.

Linda's Black Bean, but Better

Julie's mother's famous soup!

Black beans contain prebiotic fiber, which feeds beneficial gut bacteria, helps improve digestion, and maintains overall gut health. Beans contribute to a feeling of fullness and aid in weight management. Black beans are also rich in potassium, a mineral that promotes healthy blood pressure by counteracting the negative effects of sodium. Cumin can help stimulate the secretion of digestive enzymes, aiding in the breakdown of food and improving digestion. Cumin may reduce bloating and flatulence. The compounds in cumin can help soothe the digestive tract and alleviate symptoms of indigestion, such as heartburn and stomach pain. Cumin also contains beneficial prebiotic fiber. Oregano boasts a range of potential health benefits, thanks to its rich composition of antioxidants and antimicrobial compounds like carvacrol and thymol, which fight harmful free radicals that contribute to chronic diseases. Oregano also exhibits potential antibacterial and antifungal properties, which can aid in the fight against foodborne illnesses and infections. Oregano may help regulate blood sugar levels and reduce inflammation, helping to alleviate cough and muscle spasms.

(Continued)

Makes 4 servings

Ingredients:
8 ounces dry black beans
1 carrot, chopped
1 onion, peeled and chopped
1 red pepper, chopped
2 garlic cloves, peeled and minced
2 tablespoons olive oil
1 teaspoon dried oregano
1 teaspoon cumin
¼ teaspoon cayenne pepper
1 teaspoon kosher salt
½ teaspoon black pepper
1 pound pork loin cut into 1-inch chunks
1 cup red wine
¼ cup red wine vinegar
4 cups chicken stock
1 teaspoon orange zest
Orange Salsa (see recipe below)

Directions:
The day before making the soup, prepare the beans: sort through them, removing any small pebbles. Then soak the beans in cold water overnight. The next day, drain the beans and set aside.

Sauté the carrot, onion, pepper, and garlic in the olive oil over low heat about 10 minutes. Sprinkle in the oregano, cumin, cayenne, salt, and pepper. Continue gently sautéing for a few minutes. Place this veggie-spice mixture into a bowl and set aside. Turn the heat up to medium and sear the pork, turning the pieces so they brown on each side. Add red wine, red wine vinegar, chicken stock, orange zest, and black beans. Bring to a boil, then reduce to a simmer for two hours or until the beans are soft and mash to the touch. The meat should also be soft and tender.

Serve soup with a scoop of Orange Salsa.

(Continued)

Orange Salsa

Ingredients:
3 oranges, peeled and segmented
¼ cup diced red onion
2 jalapeños, finely diced
3 tablespoons lime juice
½ teaspoon kosher salt

Optional:
¼ cup chopped cilantro

Directions:
Cut each orange segment into 3 or 4 pieces.

In a small bowl, stir together the oranges, red onion, jalapeños, lime juice, salt, and cilantro (if using). Let salsa sit for 1 hour. Use leftover salsa with tacos or quesadillas.

Respiratory System

The respiratory system, responsible for the intake of oxygen and the expulsion of carbon dioxide, plays a crucial role in disease prevention. One of the primary ways the respiratory system prevents disease is by acting as a physical barrier. The nasal passages and airways are lined with mucous membranes that trap and filter inhaled particles, including dust, pollen, and pathogens. These particles are then expelled from the body through coughing or sneezing. Additionally, the cilia, tiny hairlike structures in the airways, move upward to transport mucus and trapped particles back to the throat, where they can be swallowed or expelled.

Beyond its physical barrier function, the respiratory system also plays a vital role in our defense. The lungs are home to a variety of immune cells, including macrophages, neutrophils, and lymphocytes. These cells specialize in detecting and attacking pathogens that manage to breach the respiratory system's physical barrier. Macrophages engulf and destroy bacteria and other microorganisms. Neutrophils are rapidly recruited to sites of infection, where they release powerful chemicals to kill pathogens. Lymphocytes, including T cells and B cells, coordinate the immune response and produce antibodies to neutralize pathogens.

The respiratory system also plays a role in preventing respiratory infections by maintaining healthy airways. Humidity and temperature are regulated by the nasal passages and upper airways. This helps prevent the mucous membranes from drying out, which can impair their ability to trap and filter pathogens. The respiratory system produces surfactant, a substance that coats the alveoli, the tiny air sacs in the lungs. Surfactant helps to prevent the alveoli from collapsing, ensuring that the lungs can efficiently exchange oxygen and carbon dioxide.

The respiratory system also plays a role in preventing systemic diseases. Chronic respiratory infections, such as bronchitis and pneumonia, can lead to heart disease, kidney disease, and sepsis. Maintaining a healthy respiratory system reduces the risk of illness and improves the overall quality of life.

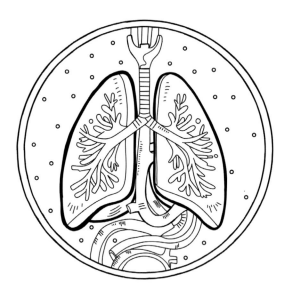

Breathe Well Chicken Soup

Chicken contains protein that provides muscle, tissue, and cellular repair during illness. When chicken cooks in soup, an amino acid called cysteine is released. Cysteine thins mucus in the lungs, aiding in chest decongestion and faster healing. Rosemary has anti-inflammatory and antioxidant properties that can help clear congestion and soothe irritated airways. Its essential oil may also act as an expectorant, loosening phlegm and promoting easier breathing. Thyme possesses potent antibacterial and antiviral properties, potentially aiding in fighting off respiratory infections and reducing inflammation. Additionally, thyme's expectorant and muscle relaxant properties can help clear mucus buildup and ease coughs, while its ability to soothe the throat can alleviate discomfort associated with respiratory issues. Ginger has long been used in traditional medicine to alleviate respiratory ailments. It contains compounds known as gingerols and shogaols, which have anti-inflammatory and antioxidant properties. These compounds can help reduce inflammation in the airways, making it easier to breathe. Additionally, ginger may help thin mucus and promote its clearance from the respiratory tract, providing relief from congestion and coughing. Ginger is a natural remedy for those seeking relief from symptoms such as common colds, bronchitis, asthma, and other upper respiratory infections.

(Continued)

Makes 4 servings

Ingredients:
2 tablespoons olive oil
1 large yellow onion, peeled and diced
2 large carrots, diced
2 stalks celery, diced
1 cup shredded cabbage
2 teaspoons turmeric
1 tablespoon fresh rosemary, finely chopped
2 tablespoons fresh thyme leaves
8 cloves fresh garlic, minced
2 tablespoons fresh ginger root, peeled and minced
4 cups chicken stock
1 pound whole chicken breasts
1 cup fresh or frozen peas
Sea salt and black pepper, to taste

Optional:
Gluten-free egg noodles (see Specialty Ingredients, page 215) or cooked rice Hot peppers

Directions:
In a large stockpot over medium-high heat, add olive oil, then onion, carrots, celery, and cabbage. Cook until slightly softened, about 10 minutes. Add turmeric, rosemary, thyme, garlic, and ginger. Continue to cook for another 5 minutes. Add the stock and place the whole chicken breasts into the soup. Reduce heat and gently simmer for 30 minutes. Remove the chicken and shred it into bite-size pieces. Add the chicken back to the soup. Add the peas and continue to simmer. Adjust the flavor with salt, pepper, and hot pepper (if desired). To make a heartier meal, add noodles or cooked rice, and simmer gently until noodles are cooked.

Fennel and Leek with Thyme

Both fennel and leeks offer potential benefits for the respiratory system thanks to their vitamins, phytonutrients, and essential oils. Fennel seeds contain compounds with potential expectorant properties, which can help loosen mucus and clear congestion, making breathing easier. This can be particularly beneficial for individuals suffering from coughs, colds, or other respiratory issues. Fennel may relax bronchial muscles, easing symptoms of asthma and bronchitis. Its potential antibacterial properties might also contribute to fighting off respiratory infections.

Leek's rich antioxidant profile, particularly flavonoids, can help combat oxidative stress, which is implicated in respiratory diseases like asthma and bronchitis. Sulfur-containing compounds in leeks can help thin mucus, making it easier to expel from the lungs. Leeks also contain anti-inflammatory properties that may soothe the airways. The vegetable's high water content helps keep the respiratory tract hydrated, which can thin mucus and prevent dryness that can irritate the airways and worsen respiratory symptoms. Both fennel and leeks are good sources of vitamin C, a potent antioxidant that strengthens the immune system, potentially reducing the risk of respiratory infections.

(Continued)

Makes 2–4 servings

Ingredients:
2 leeks
2 tablespoons olive oil
1 stalk celery, sliced
2 bulbs fresh fennel, diced
1 tablespoon fresh thyme leaves
4 cups vegetable stock
Sea salt and black pepper, to taste

Garnish:
Soup Croutons (page 209)
Chopped fennel fronds (the feathery part on top)
Fresh thyme leaves

Directions:
Remove the outermost green leaves of the leeks (save these leaves for future stock). Thoroughly rinse the leeks and slice in circles. In a large, heavy soup pot, warm the olive oil on low-medium heat. Add the sliced leeks and gently stir. Cover the pot and sweat the leeks (gently simmer) for 5 minutes, stirring once. Add the celery, fennel, and chopped thyme leaves and sauté for 5 minutes, stirring occasionally. Add the stock and season with salt and pepper. Bring the soup to a boil, reduce heat, and then simmer, loosely covered, for 30 minutes. Cool slightly and puree in a blender. Heat and garnish soup before serving.

Shakshuka

Shakshuka is a spicy North African dish made with eggs and a variety of peppers. It's typically served for breakfast, but it's hearty enough for any meal. Peppers are rich in vitamin C, which plays a crucial role in immune function and helps fight off infections that can affect the lungs. Capsaicin, the peppers' heat source, is a mild decongestant and thins mucus, making it easier to expel. Capsaicin's heat can reduce airway congestion and inflammation. Capsaicin may also reduce pain by desensitizing nerve endings in the lungs, potentially reducing cough irritation. Eggs contain vitamin B12, which is crucial for red blood cell production. Healthy red blood cells carry oxygen throughout the body, ensuring proper lung function. B12 is involved in various bodily functions, including lung surfactant production. Surfactants coat the lung alveoli, helping to prevent them from collapsing. Parsley, high in antioxidants like vitamins C and A, may help reduce inflammation in the airways, potentially easing symptoms of asthma and bronchitis. These potent ingredients combine synergistically to help maintain a healthy respiratory system.

(Continued)

Makes 2–4 servings

Ingredients:
1 onion, diced
1 red bell pepper, diced
1 green bell pepper, diced
1 jalapeño pepper, diced
2 tablespoons olive oil
1 teaspoon sweet paprika
1 teaspoon smoked paprika
1 teaspoon ground cumin
1 teaspoon chili powder
1 teaspoon Aleppo pepper or ½ teaspoon dried hot pepper flakes
Sea salt and black pepper, to taste
1 tablespoon einkorn or rice flour
1 (14-ounce) can diced (or 2 cups fresh) tomatoes
2 cups vegetable stock
2 slices bread, torn into small cubes (see Einkorn bread in "sides" section, page 215)
4 eggs
1 bunch fresh parsley, chopped

Optional:
1 tablespoon harissa or gochujang sauce (see Specialty Ingredients, page 215)

Garnish:
Feta cheese and thinly sliced scallions

Directions:
Sauté the onion and peppers in olive oil for about 5 minutes, until soft. Sprinkle paprika varieties, cumin, chili powder, Aleppo pepper, sea salt, and flour over vegetables and stir until they are coated. Add tomatoes, hot sauce (if using), stock, and bread cubes. Simmer for 20 minutes. The bread should fall apart and almost dissolve.

To serve, poach the eggs on top of the soup and then carefully ladle out 1 to 2 eggs for each serving, or poach separately and serve on top of the soup. Sprinkle with parsley and desired garnishes.

Herbed Kefir

Kefir is known for its ability to support respiratory health, especially during the cold and flu season. Its probiotics work to balance the immune system, which can help reduce the severity and frequency of respiratory infections, asthma, and more. Its probiotic profile may benefit the lungs through the lung-gut axis, the connection between gut and lung health. The gut-lung axis suggests that improving the gut microbiome also benefits the respiratory system. Kefir's live microorganisms may naturally suppress allergic reactions and aid in changing the body's response to asthma. Asthma has been linked to the "hygiene hypothesis"—resulting when the immune system develops improperly. (One theory for this is the increase in antibiotics and caesarean births, resulting in babies being less exposed to microbiome diversity needed to develop a healthy immune system.) Kefir's powerful peptides may play a role in reducing pulmonary inflammation caused by irritants like air pollution, helping to protect and heal lung tissue. Additionally, kefir may aid in combating harmful bacteria like E. coli and salmonella. Tarragon contains flavonoids, essential oils, and other compounds that offer anti-inflammatory and antioxidant benefits, which could help reduce inflammation in the respiratory tract, easing conditions like asthma or bronchitis, and protecting cells from damage caused by harmful free radicals. This could potentially help reduce or prevent respiratory inflammation and oxidative stress. Tarragon may possess expectorant properties, which could help loosen mucus and phlegm in the respiratory tract, making it easier to cough up, helping conditions like colds or bronchitis.

(Continued)

Makes 2 servings

Ingredients:
1 cucumber, peeled and finely diced
1 tomato, finely diced
1 teaspoon sea salt
2 cups plain whole-milk kefir (see Specialty Ingredients, page 215)
2 tablespoons fresh tarragon, finely sliced
2 tablespoons fresh chives, finely sliced
2 hard-boiled eggs

Directions:
Place the cucumber and tomato in a large bowl. Sprinkle the salt on top of the cucumber and tomato and let sit for 1 to 2 hours. This will draw out some of the juice and will be part of the broth. Add the kefir and herbs and stir well. Chill for at least 1 hour. Garnish the cold soup with slices of hard-boiled eggs and more fresh herbs, if desired.

Curried Fish and Chickpea Stew

Curry is a potent blend of medicinal spices that may provide powerful benefits for the respiratory system. Turmeric is high in curcumin, which reduces inflammation throughout the body, potentially aiding in managing conditions like arthritis and digestive issues. Curcumin has the ability to reduce oxidative stress, which may help to combat cancer cell growth and protect brain health. Curcumin's antioxidant properties may combat free radical damage caused by pollution, carcinogens, and other substances, thereby reducing the risk of lung damage and other diseases caused by oxidative stress. Curcumin stimulates the production of cathelicidin antimicrobial peptide (CAMP). CAMP is a crucial component of the innate immune system, acting as a broad-spectrum defense against bacteria, viruses, and fungi, even those the body hasn't encountered before. Ginger acts as an expectorant, helping to loosen and expel mucus. Cloves have anti-inflammatory and antibacterial properties that can soothe a sore throat and fight off potential respiratory infections. Ginger has antimicrobial properties and can help clear congestion. Allicin, the pungent compound in garlic, can fight bacteria that cause lung infections and reduce inflammation in the airways.

(Continued)

Makes 2 servings

Ingredients:
1 onion, diced
2 stalks celery, diced
3 tablespoons olive oil
1 tablespoon curry powder
1 teaspoon cumin
1 teaspoon ginger powder
½ teaspoon hot pepper flakes
1 (14-ounce) can diced (or 2 cups fresh) tomatoes
1 (15-ounce) can chickpeas, drained
2 cups vegetable stock
1 (13-ounce) can unsweetened coconut milk
Sea salt and black pepper, to taste
1 pound fresh codfish, haddock, or other fleshy fish, cut into large chunks

Garnish:
Chopped fresh parsley or sliced fresh chives

Optional:
Cooked basmati rice

Directions:
In a large saucepan, sauté the onion and celery in the olive oil, over medium heat, for 5 minutes. Sprinkle in the curry, cumin, ginger, pepper flakes, and tomatoes over the vegetables, and sauté for several minutes. Add the chickpeas, stock, and coconut milk. Bring to a boil, then reduce the heat and simmer for 45 minutes. Season with salt and pepper, to taste. Add the fish last and gently simmer for another 10 minutes, until the fish is tender and flaky.

Adding a scoop of rice to each bowl creates a substantial meal. Garnish with fresh parsley or chives.

Savory Winter Stew

Cabbage is rich in antioxidants and sulfur compounds that can help protect the respiratory system from damage. Turkey is a good source of lean protein and zinc, necessary for strong immune function. Turkey is abundant in tryptophan, which helps regulate sleep, also crucial for immune health. When mustard powder is inhaled as steam through soup, it can aid the respiratory system by acting as a decongestant. Its warming sensation increases blood flow to the chest, helping loosen mucus and easing coughs. Its potential antimicrobial properties might contribute to fighting off respiratory infections. Pears contain vitamin C and other anti-inflammatory compounds that may help reduce phlegm production, potentially easing symptoms of coughs and colds, and boost the immune system, potentially helping fight off respiratory infections. Their high water content can soothe dry coughs and irritated throats. Thyme is a renowned respiratory herb that may help soothe sore throats, reduce congestion, and improve breathing with the help of its special compounds, thymol, carvacrol, linalool, and flavonoids. These compounds may help to reduce inflammation, fight infection, and soothe the throat. Raw honey's natural sweetness soothes sore throats and reduces coughing frequency. Its antibacterial properties and enzymes may help combat the underlying infection, while its antioxidant compounds potentially lessen inflammation in the airways.

See Specialty Ingredients (page 215).

(Continued)

Makes 4 servings

Ingredients:
1 large leek
1 pound Italian turkey sausage
3 tablespoons butter
4 cups cabbage, thinly sliced
2 pears, divided
2 tablespoons raw honey
2 tablespoons fresh thyme leaves
1 tablespoon mustard powder
Sea salt and black pepper, to taste
1 can white beans, drained and rinsed
4 cups chicken stock
½ cup kombucha
Sea salt

Directions:
Remove the outermost green leaves of the leek (save the leaves for future stock). Slice the leek down the middle, lengthwise. Thoroughly rinse the leek, pat dry, and slice in thin half-moons. Set aside. Over medium heat, slowly brown the sausage until completely cooked. Remove the sausage and set aside.

Melt the butter in the pan with the sausage grease. Add the leeks and cabbage, and sauté for 5 minutes. Dice one of the pears and gently add to the pot. Drizzle in the honey and sprinkle in the thyme, mustard, and black pepper. Stir well. Slice the cooked sausage into thin rounds and add to the soup with the beans, stock, and kombucha. Simmer for 30 minutes. Adjust the flavor with sea salt and black pepper. Ladle soup into bowls. Cut the remaining pear into thin slices and garnish soup with a few pieces. Drizzle with raw honey just before serving.

Scallops, Fennel & Parsley

Scallops' rich content of omega-3 fatty acids reduces inflammation, potentially easing asthma symptoms. High in vitamin B12, zinc, and selenium, scallops support the immune system, which can help fight off respiratory infections that contribute to congestion and other breathing difficulties. These nutrients also support cognitive function and thyroid function. Some good news for the heart: scallops' omega-3 fatty acids may improve heart health by lowering cholesterol, reducing blood pressure, and potentially preventing strokes. Additionally, scallops are a good source of minerals like magnesium and potassium, further supporting healthy heart function. Fennel and parsley, both members of the Apiaceae family, are rich in bioactive compounds in the form of volatile oils like anethole, fenchone, and myristicin. These volatile oils possess anti-inflammatory and antimicrobial properties, making them potential candidates for treating conditions like bronchitis and asthma. They can help reduce inflammation in the airways, making it easier to breathe. Fennel, parsley, and leeks are packed with antioxidants, including flavonoids and phenolic acids. These antioxidants can help protect the lungs from damage caused by oxidative stress, a contributing factor to respiratory diseases. By neutralizing harmful free radicals, antioxidants can help prevent inflammation and cell damage in the respiratory tract.

(Continued)

Makes 4 servings

Ingredients:
1 leek
2 tablespoons olive oil
1 celery stalk, diced
1 fresh fennel bulb, diced
4 cloves garlic, peeled and chopped
1 large potato, peeled and cubed
1 jalapeño or other hot pepper, thinly sliced and diced
8 ounces clam juice
4 cups fish or chicken stock
½ cup white wine or kombucha (see Specialty Ingredients, page 215)
2 tablespoons fresh thyme leaves
Sea salt and black pepper, to taste
1 pound sea scallops (sea scallops are preferable to bay)

Garnish:
Fresh parsley, chopped
Fresh lemon slices

Directions:
Remove the outermost green leaves of the leek (save the leaves for future stock). Slice the leek down the middle, lengthwise. Thoroughly rinse the leek, pat dry, and slice in thin half-moons. Heat a large soup pan, add the olive oil, then sauté the leek, celery, fennel, and garlic for 5 minutes. Add the potato and hot pepper, stirring well. Add the clam juice, stock, white wine, thyme, salt, and black pepper. Bring to a boil, reduce to low, and simmer for 45 minutes.

Before serving, gently reheat the soup. Add the scallops and cook for 5 minutes (3 minutes if using bay scallops). Garnish with parsley and lemon and eat immediately.

Endocrine System

If the nervous system acts as the body's conductor, the endocrine system could be the conductor's nonverbal language and gestures, sending chemical messages throughout the orchestra. These chemical messengers are called hormones, and they keep everything in harmony. The endocrine system is a network of glands that produce and secrete hormones. Hormones travel throughout the bloodstream, reaching specific organs and tissues and instructing them. These hormones regulate various bodily functions, including metabolism, growth, reproduction, and stress response. By maintaining hormonal balance, the endocrine system helps to prevent a wide range of diseases.

The endocrine system contributes to disease prevention by regulating metabolism. Hormones such as thyroid hormone and insulin control how the body converts food into energy. Imbalances in these hormones can lead to metabolic disorders like hypothyroidism or diabetes, which can increase the risk of heart disease, stroke, and other health problems. Maintaining proper thyroid hormone levels and insulin sensitivity helps prevent these metabolic diseases. Growth hormone, produced by the pituitary gland, regulates growth and development during childhood and adolescence. Growth hormone imbalances can lead to growth disorders or other health problems. The endocrine system also plays a crucial role in reproductive health. Hormones such as estrogen and testosterone regulate the reproductive system. Imbalances can lead to infertility, menstrual irregularities, and other reproductive problems. By maintaining proper hormonal balance, the endocrine system helps prevent these conditions.

The endocrine system also helps regulate the body's stress response. Hormones such as cortisol and adrenaline are released in response to stress, helping the body cope with challenging situations. However, chronic stress can lead to imbalances in these hormones, increasing the risk of various health problems, including heart disease, high blood pressure, and depression. The endocrine system also interacts with other body systems to maintain overall health. For example, hormones produced by the endocrine system help to regulate the immune system, which is essential for fighting off infections and diseases. By maintaining a healthy immune system, the endocrine system helps to prevent a wide range of illnesses. Disruptions in the endocrine system can lead to a variety of health problems. Good hormone communication means good health!

Parsnip and Kale

Kale, a leafy green superfood, is packed with vitamins and minerals that support endocrine health. Kale is packed with vitamins A, C, and K, essential for vision, thyroid function, immunity, and bone health. Vitamin C is essential for hormone synthesis and can help maintain cellular integrity. Parsnips are rich in flavonoids that help protect the endocrine glands from oxidative stress, a hormone disruptor that can lead to imbalances and contribute to diseases like hypo- or hyperthyroidism. The thyroid gland is a key player in the endocrine system, regulating metabolism and other vital functions. The fiber in parsnips and kale can help regulate blood sugar levels and benefit the pancreas. Blood sugar regulation is essential for optimal endocrine function, particularly for those with diabetes. Both vegetables contain potassium, crucial for regulating blood pressure, and folate, important for cell growth and development. Rosemary's aromatic properties may help reduce stress. Chronic stress can disrupt hormone production and balance.

Antioxidant properties in rosemary may have hormone-balancing properties, particularly for women. This could potentially help with conditions like PMS, menopause, and endometriosis. Together, parsnips, kale, and rosemary work holistically and may promote hormonal balance, support the digestive and immune systems, and contribute to overall well-being.

(Continued)

Makes 4 servings

Ingredients:
1 sweet onion, peeled, halved, and thinly sliced
4 cloves garlic, peeled and finely chopped
2 tablespoons olive oil
3 parsnips, peeled and thinly sliced
5 cups vegetable stock
1 pound red potatoes, washed and diced
1 bunch kale, de-stemmed and sliced into thin ribbons
2 teaspoons fresh rosemary, chopped
Sea salt and freshly ground pepper, to taste
½ cup heavy cream
1 tablespoon fresh lemon zest
½ cup grated Parmesan cheese

Optional:
Extra grated Parmesan cheese

Directions:
Sauté the onion and garlic in olive oil over low heat for 5 minutes. Increase to medium heat, add the parsnips, and sauté for 5 minutes more. Add the stock, potatoes, kale, rosemary, salt, and pepper. Bring to a gentle boil, then reduce heat and simmer soup for 15 minutes, until the potatoes are soft. When serving, ladle the soup into bowls, then top with cream and lemon zest. Sprinkle with Parmesan cheese, and stir well, melting the cheese.

Serve with extra Parmesan cheese on top, if desired.

Harusame (Japanese Glass Noodle Soup)

Seaweed can play a crucial role in supporting the endocrine system, particularly the thyroid gland. Seaweed is abundant in iodine, a mineral essential for the production of thyroid hormones. These hormones regulate metabolism, energy levels, growth and development, body temperature, and even mood. Iodine deficiency can lead to various thyroid disorders, including goiter (enlarged thyroid gland) and hypothyroidism, which can significantly impact overall health. Tofu's benefits on the endocrine system are primarily due to its high protein content and special compounds called isoflavones. The protein helps regulate hormone production, while isoflavones, plant-based compounds similar to estrogen, can interact with estrogen receptors in the body. This interaction can help balance hormone levels, potentially reducing symptoms like hot flashes and night sweats during menopause. Additionally, tofu's low fat content and lack of cholesterol can support overall cardiovascular health, also important for endocrine function. Tamari is a gluten-free soy sauce made from fermented soybeans and salt. Its high protein content supports muscle growth and repair. Tamari contains iron, B vitamins, and antioxidants that help to improve gut health and protect cells from damage. Also, tamari's lower sodium content compared to traditional soy sauce makes it a healthier option for those watching their sodium intake.

See Specialty Ingredients (page 215).

(Continued)

Makes 2–3 servings

Ingredients:
2 eggs
1 tablespoon water
2 teaspoons toasted sesame oil
3 scallions, thinly sliced
1–2 tablespoons tamari, to taste
1 teaspoon black pepper
1 teaspoon ground ginger
3 cups stock
3 ounces firm tofu, cubed
2 ounces harusame—cellophane (glass) noodles
2 sheets nori seaweed, cut into thin strips

Directions:
Beat the eggs with 1 tablespoon of water and set aside.

Warm the sesame oil on low heat in a large soup saucepan. Sauté the scallions for a few minutes. Add the tamari, pepper, and ginger, and stir well. Add the stock and tofu. Cook the cellophane noodles in the soup until they are *al dente* (soft but with a "bite"). Reduce the soup to a simmer. Gently pour in the beaten eggs, in a slow steady stream. When done correctly, there will be long thin strips of fluffy cooked eggs. The soup is ready when the eggs are fully cooked—a few minutes. Stir the soup in a swirling motion to break eggs into "noodles." Ladle into bowls and garnish with a heaping mound of nori strips.

Lemon Tahini

Tahini can be helpful in maintaining hormone health, particularly in women. Tahini contains lignans, a type of phytoestrogen. Lignans can mimic the effects of estrogen in the body, potentially playing a supportive role in managing hormonal changes, especially during menopause. Lignans bind to estrogen receptors, potentially alleviating symptoms like hot flashes and mood swings associated with estrogen deficiency. Lignans may bind to estrogen receptors in breast tissue, potentially reducing the risk of certain hormone-dependent cancers. Selenium, present in tahini, is crucial for thyroid hormone production and metabolism regulation. Lemons are rich in vitamin C, an antioxidant that can help protect cells from damage and reduce inflammation, associated with various endocrine disorders including thyroid dysfunction and polycystic ovary syndrome (PCOS). Additionally, lemons contain flavonoids, which may have hormone-balancing properties. Coconut oil's potential benefits for endocrine health are primarily attributed to its medium-chain triglycerides (MCTs). MCTs are metabolized differently than long-chain triglycerides, potentially supporting healthy blood sugar levels and insulin sensitivity. This can be beneficial for individuals with conditions like diabetes or metabolic syndrome.

(Continued)

Makes 4 servings

Ingredients:
1 leek
¼ cup tahini
¼ cup lemon juice
4¼ cups vegetable stock, divided
1 cup water, if needed
2 tablespoons extra-virgin olive oil
2 tablespoons coconut oil
1 stalk celery, finely chopped
1 carrot, finely chopped
8 cloves garlic, peeled and minced
1 teaspoon ground Aleppo pepper or crushed red pepper
1 tablespoon fresh thyme leaves
1 teaspoon paprika
½ cup brown rice
Sea salt, to taste

Garnish:
Thin slices of lemon

Directions:
Remove the outermost green leaves of the leek (save the leaves for future stock). Thoroughly rinse the leek and slice thinly. Set aside. In a bowl, combine the tahini, lemon juice, and ¼ cup of stock. When the mixture thickens, add the water, a little at a time, whisking until smooth and lump free. Set aside.

Melt the oils in a large heavy-bottomed saucepan on medium heat. Sauté all the vegetables until they start to soften but not brown. Add remaining ingredients. Bring to a boil, then reduce heat and simmer gently for 45 minutes, until the brown rice is cooked. Lastly, whisk in the tahini-lemon mixture. Serve hot with a lemon slice floating on top.

Cold Cherry Yogurt

Cherries have long been touted as a remedy for gout. Uric acid buildup in the body is a key factor in gout. Cherries contain anthocyanins, which help inhibit the enzyme responsible for uric acid production. Anthocyanins promote uric acid excretion through the kidneys, reduce inflammation, and improve kidney function, all of which can also help to lower uric acid levels. Anthocyanins act as antioxidants, protecting cells from damage caused by free radicals, potentially reducing the risk of chronic diseases like heart disease and certain cancers. Having trouble sleeping? Tart cherries contain melatonin, a hormone that regulates sleep-wake cycles. Drinking tart cherry juice before bed may promote better sleep quality and duration. The probiotics found in yogurt help maintain a healthy gut microbiome, which may improve insulin sensitivity. This is particularly important for individuals with type 2 diabetes, an endocrine disorder. Calcium and vitamin D are vital for proper thyroid function, and both are available in yogurt. Raw honey's potential benefits for endocrine health are attributed to its antioxidant properties and natural sugars. Antioxidants can help protect cells from oxidative stress and reduce inflammation, which is linked to various endocrine disorders. Additionally, raw honey contains fructose and glucose, which can be metabolized differently than refined sugars, potentially supporting healthy blood sugar levels and insulin sensitivity.

(Continued)

Makes 2 servings

Ingredients:
½ cup water
¼ cup raw honey
½ cup freshly squeezed orange juice or kombucha
   (see Specialty Ingredients, page 215)
Grated zest of one lemon
12 ounces fresh dark cherries, pitted (or frozen and thawed)
1 cup whole-milk Greek yogurt

GARNISH:
Additional yogurt
Whole cherries
Mint leaves

Directions:
Slowly whisk the water and raw honey together until the honey is completely dissolved. Add this mixture, plus all of the remaining ingredients, into a blender and puree. Chill at least one hour before serving. Before serving, the soup may have to be remixed, if the liquid and yogurt separate.

Savory Wild Rice and Apple Chowder

Wild rice is a good source of alpha lipoic acid (ALA), a type of omega-3 fatty acid. ALA may help improve insulin sensitivity, helping the body's cells to better respond to the insulin hormone. This can be beneficial to people with type 2 diabetes. It may boost the body's ability to produce insulin and reduce the symptoms of diabetic nerve damage. ALA may influence cell-signaling pathways involved in hormone production and regulation. ALA also plays a role in metabolism, including the breakdown of fats and carbohydrates. This can indirectly affect hormone levels, as metabolic imbalances can impact hormone production and regulation. Apples have a positive effect on blood sugar management. Apples are high in soluble fiber, which helps slow down the absorption of sugar into the bloodstream, preventing those sharp spikes often associated with sugary foods.

Like most grains, wild rice is high in nutrients and fiber, contributing to feelings of fullness, helping with weight management. One micronutrient abundant in wild rice is manganese, an antioxidant that plays a role in keeping the mitochondria healthy. Mitochondria are the "power sources" of cells, providing energy for the cell to function. Manganese plays a role in maintaining a healthy metabolism. Wild rice is dark in color, which indicates its high antioxidant content. It contains apigenin, an antioxidant that may have anticancer properties by inhibiting the growth and proliferation of cancer cells.

(Continued)

Makes 4 servings

Ingredients:
6 tablespoons butter or coconut oil
1 onion, peeled and diced
1 carrot, diced
¼ cup einkorn, oat, or gluten-free flour (see Specialty Ingredients, page 215)
3 cups vegetable stock
1 large firm apple (like Granny Smith), peeled and cubed
2 cups cooked wild rice
½ teaspoon salt
1 cup whole milk or nondairy milk

Garnish:
3 tablespoons sliced almonds

Directions:
Melt the butter or oil in a heavy-bottomed saucepan. Sauté the onion and carrot for several minutes, until they soften. Sprinkle in the flour and continue to cook for a few minutes, stirring constantly. Slowly add the stock, whisking gently but steadily, to prevent any flour lumps. Add the apple, cooked wild rice, and salt to taste. Bring to a gentle boil, then reduce the heat quickly and simmer the soup for 15 minutes, until the apples are very soft.

Just before serving, add the milk and reheat (do not boil). Sprinkle almonds on top of each bowl.

Korean Salmon Miso

Salmon and soy offer a powerful duo for supporting hormonal health. Salmon, rich in omega-3 fatty acids, particularly DHA, plays a crucial role in regulating hormone production. These healthy fats help maintain cell membrane fluidity, which is essential for proper hormone signaling. These special fats help your brain cells talk to each other better, which is important for learning, memory, and even reducing the risk of brain fog. These fatty acids also help fight off inflammation, which can damage brain cells and contribute to conditions like depression and dementia. Salmon oil is indicated for people with ADHD and other neurodivergent issues. In addition to the fatty acids, salmon is a good source of vitamin D and other nutrients that may help the brain regulate dopamine and serotonin, which can have a calming effect. Omega-3 fatty acids may also help reduce anxiety and depression. Tamari, miso, and edamame are all soy products. Soy contains plant compounds called isoflavones, which have mild estrogen-like effects. Isoflavones help balance estrogen levels in the body, potentially alleviating symptoms associated with hormonal imbalances, particularly during menopause.

See Specialty Ingredients (page 215).

(Continued)

Makes 2–4 servings

Ingredients:
1 tablespoon raw honey
1 tablespoon freshly squeezed lemon juice
4 tablespoons tamari, divided
8-ounce salmon fillet, skin-on
2 tablespoons fresh ginger root, peeled and minced
3 cups vegetable stock
½ cup frozen edamame
2 heads bok choy, thinly sliced
2 scallions, thinly sliced
⅓ cup miso

Garnish:
Sesame seeds

Directions:
Whisk together honey, lemon juice, and 2 tablespoons of the tamari in a medium bowl. Add the salmon and coat on all sides. Marinate at room temperature for 10 minutes, turning salmon occasionally. Place the salmon skin-side down on a lined baking sheet. Preheat the oven to broil, setting the rack 4 inches from the upper heat source. Broil the salmon until just cooked through, 4 to 8 minutes, depending on the thickness of the fillet. Let it cool, and then gently break salmon apart into bite-size pieces. Set aside.

When salmon is ready, place ginger, remaining tamari, and stock in a saucepan. Heat until very warm. Add edamame, bok choy, and scallions and simmer for a few minutes, until the bok choy starts to soften. Just before serving, add the miso: In a separate bowl, dissolve the miso with some of the soup's broth, then add this mixture into the soup and stir well. Ladle into bowls, add salmon, sprinkle with sesame seeds, and serve immediately.

Happy Baby

Sweet potatoes and chickpeas offer a holistic combination that provides essential benefits for pregnant women. They contain valuable nutrients like magnesium, potassium, protein, and iron, which aid muscle and nerve function for healthy growth and development. Iron helps prevent anemia, a common concern during pregnancy due to increased blood volume. Potassium helps regulate blood pressure, which can be a concern during pregnancy. Magnesium is essential to support fetal growth and development. It plays a crucial role in various bodily functions, including muscle and nerve function, blood pressure regulation, and energy production. Adequate magnesium intake can help reduce the risk of preterm labor, preeclampsia, and gestational diabetes. Sweet potatoes contain vitamin A, crucial for healthy fetal development, particularly for vision and organ formation. Chickpeas contain folate, a critical nutrient for preventing neural tube defects in the developing baby. Coconut milk can be a beneficial addition to a pregnant woman's diet. It is a good source of healthy fats, which are essential for fetal brain development. Both sweet potatoes and chickpeas are high in fiber, promoting digestive health and helping to prevent constipation, another common pregnancy concern.

(Continued)

Makes 4 servings

Ingredients:
1 onion, peeled and chopped
2 tablespoons coconut oil
1 red bell pepper, diced
1 sweet potato, scrubbed and diced
3 cups vegetable stock
1 can light coconut milk
1 can chickpeas, drained and rinsed
1 teaspoon tamari (or sea salt, to taste)
Black pepper, to taste
2 packed cups spinach

Garnish:
Chopped lacto-fermented dill pickles or other pickled veggies

Directions:
In a heavy-bottomed saucepan, sauté the onion in oil on medium heat for a few minutes, stirring occasionally, until it softens. Add the red bell pepper and continue sautéing for a few minutes. Add the sweet potato, stock, coconut milk, and chickpeas. Bring to a boil, then reduce heat and simmer for 30 minutes, until the sweet potato is fork-tender. Adjust the seasoning with tamari and black pepper. Right before serving, heat the soup just to a boil, and then quickly add the spinach. Cook until the spinach is barely wilted—barely one minute.

Garnish with pickles if you crave them!

Integumentary System

The integumentary system is an "external guardian" made up of multiple parts that come together to perform a specific function. The integumentary system is considered a complex organ, and it is the largest organ in the human body.

While one organ, it is made up of several parts, including the hair, skin, nails, sweat glands, and sensory receptors. These are the body's first line of defense against disease, providing a physical barrier that protects against pathogens and harmful environmental factors. The skin's outermost layer, the epidermis, is a tough, keratinized (protein) surface that prevents the entry of bacteria, viruses, fungi, and other microorganisms. This barrier is constantly being renewed, helping to maintain its integrity and effectiveness. Additionally, the skin contains natural oils and sweat that create an acidic environment, which inhibits the growth of many pathogens.

The skin is home to a variety of immune cells, including Langerhans cells and dendritic cells. These specialize in detecting and capturing pathogens that attempt to breach the skin's barrier. Once a pathogen is captured, these cells can present it to other immune cells, triggering an immune response that helps to eliminate the infection. The integumentary system also plays a vital role in preventing skin cancer. The skin contains melanocytes, cells that produce melanin, a pigment that absorbs harmful ultraviolet (UV) radiation from the sun. Melanin helps to protect the skin from the DNA damage caused by UV radiation, which can lead to skin cancer. The integumentary system also plays a role in preventing other skin diseases, such as infections and allergies. While the skin's barrier helps prevent infections by keeping pathogens out, the skin's immune cells can help to fight off infections that breach the barrier. The skin can also react to allergens by triggering allergic reactions, such as hives or eczema. These reactions help to remove the allergen from the body and prevent further exposure.

Beyond protection, the integumentary system plays a vital role in maintaining homeostasis, the body's internal balance. It helps regulate fluid loss through sweat and prevents excessive water loss. Additionally, the skin is involved in the synthesis of vitamin D. Vitamin D plays a crucial role in supporting a healthy immune system, helping regulate the body's response to infections and diseases. It is also essential for calcium absorption and bone health. Vitamin D is produced when the skin is exposed to sunlight; therefore, sun exposure is important—in moderation.

Finally, the integumentary system contributes to our sense of self and identity. Skin color, texture, and appearance are unique and play a significant role in how we perceive ourselves and how others perceive us. Skin conditions such as acne or eczema can have a negative impact on our self-esteem. Healthy skin can contribute to a healthy quality of life.

Green Cleanse

Greens, like spinach, are powerhouses for maintaining a healthy integumentary system. Spinach is packed with antioxidants like vitamins A, C, and E, which combat free radicals that damage skin cells, contributing to wrinkles and premature aging. These antioxidants also protect against sun damage, potentially reducing the risk of skin cancer. Vitamin C is crucial for creating collagen, a protein that provides skin with its structure and elasticity, leading to a firmer, younger-looking appearance. It helps produce white blood cells to fight off infections and also helps neutralize harmful free radicals that can damage cells and contribute to skin cancer. Spinach's high water content helps promote skin hydration, reducing dryness and irritation. Greens also contain anti-inflammatory compounds that can help soothe irritated skin and reduce conditions like acne and eczema. Additionally, broccoli contains compounds called glucosinolates, which break down into isothiocyanates. These have been shown to have anti-cancer properties, including skin cancer prevention. The piperine in black pepper can help neutralize harmful free radicals, which can contribute to skin damage and premature aging. Piperine can enhance the absorption of other nutrients and compounds. Additionally, black pepper may have anti-inflammatory properties, which can help reduce skin inflammation and promote sweating, to help detoxify the body. Not bad, for a big green bowl!

(Continued)

Makes 2 servings

Ingredients:
1¼ cups fresh broccoli florets
2 cups fresh spinach, firmly packed
3 cloves garlic, chopped
1 tablespoon fresh ginger root, peeled and chopped
½ teaspoon turmeric
¼ teaspoon cayenne pepper
1 cup vegetable stock
½ cup coconut milk
1 tablespoon freshly squeezed lemon juice
Sea salt and freshly ground black pepper, to taste

Garnish:
Plain yogurt or kefir
Lemon slices
Roasted pumpkin seeds

Directions:
Lightly steam broccoli florets. Set aside ¼ cup broccoli for garnish.

Place the spinach, broccoli, and remaining ingredients into a blender. Puree until smooth. If necessary, stop the blender and stir the ingredients to dislodge the blade, then remix. Pour soup into a saucepan and heat until hot, but not to boiling.

Pour into a bowl, top with remaining broccoli florets, and add the garnish.

Watermelon Gazpacho

Watermelon offers several benefits for the hair, skin, and nails. First off, watermelon is mostly water—over 90 percent! It provides natural hydration for the skin, eliminates toxins, and reduces the appearance of fine lines and wrinkles. Watermelon boasts antioxidants and anti-inflammatory compounds like vitamins A and C, and lycopene, which promote collagen, combat free radical damage, help soothe skin irritation and redness, and prevent damage caused by the sun. Collagen is critical to skin health, keeping it elastic, smooth, and supple. Watermelon is a rich source of lycopene. Lycopene may help protect the skin from the harmful effects of ultraviolet (UV) radiation, reducing the risk of sunburn and long-term damage like premature aging and skin cancer. Lycopene may help reduce inflammation in the skin, which is linked to various skin conditions such as acne, eczema, and psoriasis. A healthy skin barrier helps protect the skin from irritants and moisture loss. Lycopene may help strengthen the skin barrier, leading to smoother, healthier-looking skin.

(Continued)

Makes 2–4 servings

Ingredients:
1 pound watermelon, rind removed, cubed
1 large organic cucumber (or peeled if there is a waxy coating), sliced
Juice of 1 freshly squeezed lime
1 red onion, peeled and diced
½ cup Greek olives, diced

Garnish:
Feta cheese
Chopped fresh mint
Jalapeños, thinly sliced

Directions:
Tajín or other citrus-chili seasoning (see Specialty Ingredients, page 215)

This soup is fast and easy to put together. While there is no cooking, it should be prepared right before serving. The secret to this soup is in its garnish.

Place the watermelon in a blender and puree. To help the process, stop the blender occasionally, and push the fruit down into the pureed mixture with a wooden spoon. Continue this a few times until the melon is the consistency of a smooth liquid. Next, add the cucumber and lime juice and puree again. That's it!

Ladle into bowls, add the red onion and olives, and then add the garnish: a scoop of feta cheese, fresh mint, and jalapeño. If desired, sprinkle with Tajín seasoning.

Pesto Pasta Stew

Olive oil plays a key role in this soup, and in skin health, in general. Olive oil is rich in squalane and vitamin E. Squalane helps skin retain moisture, while vitamin E boosts the skin's ability to absorb and utilize water. This combination keeps skin hydrated and supple. Olive oil's antioxidants, vitamin E, and polyphenols help fight free radicals, which can damage skin cells. The emollient properties of olive oil can help soothe dry, itchy, or irritated skin. It may also provide some relief for conditions like eczema and psoriasis. Spinach offers several medicinal benefits for the skin cells, thanks to its rich content of vitamins A, C, and K, along with iron and magnesium. Vitamin A promotes skin cell turnover and collagen production, reducing wrinkles and fine lines. Vitamin C acts as an antioxidant, protecting the skin from damage. Vitamin K helps improve blood circulation, which can enhance skin tone and reduce dark circles. Vitamin K is crucial for red blood cell production, healthy blood clotting, and bruise prevention. The iron supports healthy red blood cells, ensuring adequate oxygen delivery to the skin. Spinach is an excellent source of folate, important for cell repair and renewal, which contributes to healthy hair and nail growth.

(Continued)

Makes 4–6 servings

Ingredients:

Spinach Pesto:
4 ounces (3 cups) fresh spinach (stems can be included)
¼ cup olive oil
¼ cup grated Parmesan cheese

Optional:
1 tablespoon water

Soup:
1 onion, peeled and chopped
2 tablespoons olive oil
6 cups vegetable stock
½ cup einkorn or gluten-free pasta, such as rotini or fusilli
½ cup fresh or frozen peas
½ cup fresh green beans, sliced into 1-inch chunks
1 zucchini, diced
2 tablespoons miso

Directions:

Prepare the spinach pesto: Place the spinach, olive oil, and Parmesan cheese in a food processor. Start by pulsing the machine, and then puree the ingredients well. Add a tablespoon of water for a smoother texture. Set aside.

Prepare the soup: Sauté the onions in olive oil on medium heat for 5 minutes. Add the stock and bring to a boil. Add the pasta and cook for 5 minutes. Add the green vegetables and cook for another 5 minutes. Turn off the heat. In a separate bowl, dissolve the miso with some of the soup's broth, then add this mixture into the soup and stir well. Ladle into bowls and garnish with a healthy scoop of spinach pesto.

Chilled Cucumber Avocado

Cucumbers, with their high water content (around 96 percent), act as a natural hydrator, helping to keep the skin plump and supple, thereby reducing the appearance of fine lines and wrinkles. Additionally, cucumber's cooling properties can soothe inflammation and irritation, making them a popular remedy for sunburns and puffy eyes—both internally (when eaten) and externally (applied directly to the skin).

Avocados are packed with healthy fats like monounsaturated fatty acids, which help maintain the skin's natural moisture barrier, also preventing dryness and irritation. Avocados contain vitamin E, a powerful antioxidant that reduces signs of aging while protecting skin cells from damage caused by free radicals, potentially helping with eczema, psoriasis, skin blemishes, and some skin cancers. Parsley and lime juice contain helpful nutrients like vitamin C and flavonoids, which have anti-inflammatory properties that can help reduce redness and irritation. Additionally, the chlorophyll in parsley may have natural bleaching properties, making it a potential remedy for hyperpigmentation. The hydrating properties of cucumber, the nourishing fats of avocado, and the anti-inflammatory properties of parsley and lime juice work synergistically to keep the skin hydrated, supple, and youthful. Enjoy this soup to promote healthy skin!

(Continued)

Makes 2 servings

Ingredients:
1 large English cucumber, chopped
1 ripe avocado, cut into chunks
1 jalapeño pepper, chopped
3 tablespoons freshly squeezed lime juice
1 bunch parsley, chopped
½ teaspoon sea salt
¼ cup water, optional

Garnish:
Fresh diced pineapple
Diced cucumber
Tajín seasoning (see Specialty Ingredients, page 215)

Directions:
Place all ingredients into a food processor or blender and mix until smooth. Add the water if soup is too thick. Ladle into bowl and garnish with diced pineapple and cucumber. Sprinkle with Tajín.

Celery Chowder

Celery is a good source of electrolytes like sodium and potassium. These minerals play a crucial role in maintaining proper fluid balance in the body, which is essential for healthy skin. Anti-inflammatory compounds like luteolin and apigenin can help soothe skin irritation, redness, and potentially alleviate symptoms of inflammatory skin conditions like eczema and psoriasis. Celery contains vitamin C and flavonoids, powerful antioxidants that combat free radical damage. This damage can contribute to premature aging and skin conditions like wrinkles and brown spots. Celery is about 95 percent water, which helps keep the skin hydrated and plump, reducing the appearance of fine lines and wrinkles. Cabbage contains sulfur, a mineral that helps form keratin, a protein essential for healthy skin, hair, and nails. This can contribute to overall skin health and potentially improve its texture and strength. Cabbage is a powerhouse of vitamin C, a potent antioxidant that fights free radicals. Vitamin C also plays a crucial role in the production of collagen, the protein that gives skin its structure and elasticity, leading to a firmer, younger-looking appearance. Tarragon's anti-inflammatory compound, phenolic acid, may reduce pain associated with conditions like osteoarthritis. Tarragon can affect GABA, a protein in the body that helps improve sleep quality and regulate sleep patterns.

(Continued)

Makes 4 servings

Ingredients:
2 tablespoons butter or olive oil
1½ cups celery, chopped
1 cup cabbage, chopped
1 onion, peeled and chopped
1 potato, peeled and diced
1 teaspoon tamari (see Specialty Ingredients, page 215)
¼ teaspoon white pepper
2 tablespoons fresh tarragon
4 cups vegetable stock

Garnish:
Thinly-sliced celery
Soup Croutons (page 209)

Directions:
In a large pot, melt the butter over medium heat. Sauté the celery, cabbage, and onion for 5 minutes. Add the diced potato, tamari, and spices, and sauté for 5 minutes more. Pour in the vegetable stock and stir well. Bring the mixture to a boil, reduce heat, and simmer for 30 minutes, until the vegetables are tender. Blend the soup until partially smooth and still a little chunky. An immersion blender works well for this; if using a standing blender, be careful to avoid hot splatters!

Garnish just before serving.

Creamy Cauliflower

Cauliflower's bounty of super-nutrients increases overall health in the entire body and aids in the maintenance of healthy skin. Cauliflower is a member of the Brassica family that includes broccoli, cauliflower, and kale. Brassicas are rich in antioxidants and phytochemicals that may reduce inflammation, improve heart health, and decrease the risk of certain types of cancer, including melanomas. Brassicas contain compounds called glucosinolates, which break down into isothiocyanates when the vegetables are chewed and cooked (and pureed). These isothiocyanates may have anti-inflammatory and anticancer properties. Brassicas also contain indoles, which can help regulate estrogen levels. High levels of estrogen may increase the risk of certain cancers, including melanomas. Cauliflower contains vitamins C and K, plus compounds like sulforaphane and indole-3-carbinol, which reduce inflammation and may help in fighting cancer. Turmeric contains curcumin, a potent anti-inflammatory and antioxidant compound. Turmeric also contains choline and folate, which may boost brain function. Together, they offer a powerful combination: cauliflower provides essential nutrients and potential cancer-fighting properties, while turmeric combats inflammation throughout the body.

(Continued)

Makes 4 servings

Ingredients:
1 head cauliflower, broken into large florets
2 tablespoons high-heat vegetable oil, such as grapeseed or avocado
½ teaspoon sea salt
1 large onion, roughly chopped
¼ cup olive oil, plus more for drizzling, divided
4 cloves garlic, roughly chopped
1 teaspoon cumin
1 teaspoon turmeric
4 cups vegetable stock
Sea salt and black pepper, to taste

Garnish:
Soup Croutons (page 209)
Thin slice of lemon
Olive oil

Directions:
Preheat the oven to 450°F. Line an edged baking sheet with parchment paper or aluminum foil for easier cleanup. Spread cauliflower florets on the baking sheet and drizzle with the vegetable oil. Toss cauliflower in the oil to coat, and then sprinkle with salt. Bake for 15 to 20 minutes. Some of the edges should be dark brown. The cauliflower will not be completely fork tender at this point. Set aside.

In a cast-iron saucepan, sauté the onion in the olive oil for about 5 minutes. Add the garlic and continue sautéing for another 5 minutes. Stir frequently to keep the garlic from burning. Add the cumin and turmeric and cook for another minute. Next, add the cauliflower and stock. Bring the mixture to a boil, then reduce and simmer for about 30 minutes, until cauliflower is tender. Puree the soup with a blender, being careful to avoid hot splatters.

Before serving, garnish with croutons, lemon, and a drizzle of olive oil

Soup Sides

Einkorn Pumpkin Bread

Einkorn, an ancient wheat variety, has a simpler genetic makeup than its modern relative—only fourteen chromosomes compared to modern wheat's forty-two. This translates to a more easily digested grain, especially for people with gluten sensitivity. While einkorn isn't gluten-free, its different gluten structure makes it potentially more tolerable. Einkorn is more nutritious, too—higher levels of protein, fiber, and minerals like zinc and magnesium. It contains significantly more beta-carotene, a precursor to vitamin A, which helps boost the immune system and may protect against heart disease and certain cancers. Einkorn also boasts higher levels of lutein, an antioxidant that can help prevent macular degeneration and cataracts. Einkorn may be good news for diabetics and people looking to manage their blood sugar. Its starch structure differs from modern wheat, containing higher amounts of amylose, a slowly digested starch, compared to amylopectin, which breaks down quickly and causes blood sugar spikes. This slower digestion creates gradual rises in blood sugar levels after consuming einkorn products. The glycemic index (GI) ranks carbohydrates based on their impact on blood sugar. Einkorn's starch composition suggests a potentially lower GI compared to modern wheat. Einkorn also delivers a unique flavor profile with a nutty and slightly sweet taste, adding another dimension to baked goods.

See Specialty Ingredients (page 215).

(Continued)

Makes about 12 servings

Ingredients:
3½ cups all-purpose einkorn flour*
2 teaspoons baking soda
½ teaspoon baking powder
1 teaspoon cinnamon
1 teaspoon salt
1 (15-ounce) can pumpkin puree or 2 cups fresh mashed pumpkin
¾ cup unsalted butter, melted and cooled
⅔ cup warm water
3 large eggs
1½ cups coconut sugar or other unrefined sugar

Directions:
Spray two 9 × 5-inch loaf pans with cooking spray and set aside. In a large bowl, whisk together the flour, baking soda, baking powder, cinnamon, and salt. In a separate bowl, mix pumpkin puree, butter, and warm water. Add eggs to pumpkin mixture, stirring continuously until well combined. Add sugar and mix well. Add dry ingredients 1 cup at a time, stirring until just combined. Be careful to avoid overmixing. Wrap the loaf pans and allow the dough to rest for an hour or few in the refrigerator. This allows the einkorn flour time to absorb the liquid. Afterward, divide batter into the two loaf pans. Turn the oven on 350°F (no preheating) and bake for 50 to 60 minutes. Test for doneness by inserting a toothpick into the loaf. When the bread is done, a few crumbs will still cling to the toothpick. Let bread cool in the pan for 15 minutes, and then remove loaves onto a cooling rack.

Enjoy this bread with any of the savory soup recipes.

---

* For the most accurate measurement, sift the einkorn flour before measuring it.

Sprouted Cornbread Muffins

Corn has long been hailed as a superfood for endurance and stamina. The Tarahumara, an indigenous people living in the mountainous Copper Canyons of Mexico who have eaten pinole corn for centuries, are known for their amazing athletic abilities. Drinking a roasted ground corn beverage, they are purported to run more than twenty-five miles a day! (Pinole is a traditional food made from ground cornmeal, often mixed with chia seeds, agave nectar, dates, and cinnamon.) These "running people" can tackle distances of 50 to 100 miles, seemingly effortlessly, often for enjoyment or during traditional hunts. Spelt is considered more digestible than its modern wheat "cousin" (see Einkorn Pumpkin Bread recipe description on the previous page). Furthermore, the sprouting process activates enzymes that help break down a grain's complex nutrients into easily digestible forms, making them more bioavailable to the body. Flaxseed is a rich source of fiber, omega-3 fatty acids, lignans, and antioxidants. Omega-3s support heart health and may reduce inflammation and improve brain function. Lignans are phytoestrogens, plant-based compounds that mimic the effects of estrogen in the body. Lignans have potential hormone-balancing properties. Fiber aids digestion and manages blood sugar levels.

Substitutions are listed in the recipe.

See Specialty Ingredients (page 215).

(Continued)

Makes about 12 muffins

Ingredients:
1 tablespoon flaxseed
3 tablespoons water
1¼ cups organic cornmeal
¾ cup sprouted spelt flour
1 teaspoon baking powder
½ teaspoon baking soda
½ teaspoon salt
1½ cups almond or other nondairy milk
3 tablespoons honey or maple syrup
4 tablespoons olive oil or coconut oil
1 cup fresh or frozen corn kernels (completely thawed, if frozen)

Optional:
½ cup grated cheese
Diced poblano peppers

Directions:
Preheat oven to 375°F. Line a regular-sized muffin pan.

Prepare the flaxseed egg substitute: combine ground flaxseed with water and stir. Let it sit for five minutes to thicken. Set aside.

In one bowl, whisk together the dry ingredients: cornmeal, sprouted spelt flour, baking powder, baking soda, and salt. In a larger second bowl, whisk together the wet ingredients: flax egg substitute, almond milk, honey, and olive oil. Add the corn kernels (and cheese or peppers if using) and whisk once more. Add the dry ingredients all at once into the wet ingredients. Quickly stir in until just combined. Spoon immediately into the prepared muffin tins. Bake for 18 to 22 minutes, until an inserted toothpick comes out clean. Remove from muffin pans after 15 minutes.

Cool completely before eating.

Enjoy these muffins with any of the savory or sweet soup recipes.

Herby Biscuits

Chives are related to garlic, and so they also contain allicin, a super-antioxidant believed to combat aging. Chives are rich in the nutrients beta-carotene, potassium, and vitamin K. Dill contains high amounts of vitamin A, which supports eye health. It's also known for potential digestive benefits and may help manage blood sugar and cholesterol levels. Coconut oil offers several potential health benefits, including improved heart health due to its high levels of saturated fats that may increase HDL cholesterol ("good" cholesterol). It can also aid digestion by acting as a prebiotic, supporting healthy gut bacteria. Coconut oil might help boost metabolism due to its medium-chain triglycerides (MCTs). These MCTs are absorbed and metabolized more quickly than long-chain triglycerides found in other oils. Additionally, coconut oil has antimicrobial properties, potentially fighting off harmful bacteria and viruses.

See Einkorn Pumpkin Bread (page 185) for information on einkorn.

See Specialty Ingredients (page 215).

Makes about 12 biscuits

Ingredients:

2 cups einkorn or gluten-free AP flour
1 tablespoon baking powder
1 teaspoon baking soda
1 teaspoon sea salt
¼ cup coconut oil or butter, chilled
1 cup plain sour cream, cold
2 tablespoons fresh dill, finely chopped
2 tablespoons fresh chives, sliced

(Continued)

Directions:

Preheat the oven to 400°F. In a medium mixing bowl, whisk together the flour, baking powder, baking soda, and salt. Add the cold coconut oil in small scoops and "cut" into the flour mixture with a fork or pastry cutter, until the texture looks like course cornmeal. Add the sour cream and herbs, lightly stirring until it starts to hold together. Scrape the dough onto a lightly floured counter, and sprinkle flour on top of the dough. Quickly and gently form into a ball. Fold dough over and onto itself a few times. Pat the dough ball into a circle, about 1 inch thick. Cut out biscuits with a 2½-inch-round cutter or upside-down glass. Keep the cutter straight when cutting biscuits to help them rise evenly. After cutting all the biscuits from the dough circle, gently push the scraps together and keep forming biscuits until the dough is all formed. Bake on an ungreased baking sheet for 15 minutes.

Best enjoyed while warm.

Enjoy these biscuits with any of the savory soup recipes.

Easy Yogurt Flatbread

Gluten-free flour works well for flatbread, since there is minimal dough rising needed. Dough rising typically relies on wheat's gluten. Gluten, a protein found in wheat, barley, and other grains, can cause significant health problems for individuals with celiac disease. This autoimmune disorder triggers an immune response that damages the small intestine, leading to malabsorptio of nutrients. Symptoms include diarrhea, bloating, fatigue, and weight loss. Non-celiac gluten sensitivity (NCGS) is another condition characterized by similar digestive issues and other symptoms like headaches and joint pain. The book *Wheat Belly* posits that modern wheat is a primary culprit in a range of health issues. The author argues that the hybridization of wheat has transformed the grain into having a high glycemic index, leading to insulin resistance, weight gain, and type 2 diabetes. Additionally, it claims that wheat-derived proteins can trigger inflammation and autoimmune responses, contributing to conditions like heart disease, arthritis, and digestive problems. The book emphasizes the role of wheat in fostering a "toxic" internal environment, ultimately impacting overall health and well-being.

Slather flatbread with extra yogurt for its probiotic benefits!

(Continued)

Makes about 6 servings

Ingredients:
1½ cups gluten-free flour (see Specialty Ingredients, page 215)
2 teaspoons baking powder
½ teaspoon salt
4 garlic cloves, peeled and finely chopped
¾ cup plain whole-milk Greek yogurt

OPTIONAL GARNISH:
Fresh chopped herbs

Directions:
Add all the ingredients together in a large bowl in the order listed. Begin by stirring with a wooden spoon and then knead the dough by hand until it forms a smooth ball. Continue kneading for 5 minutes. Sprinkle the dough with a bit of flour if it is sticky. Cover the dough and let rest for 1–4 hours. Divide the dough into 8 even balls. Press each ball into a rough circle approximately 6 inches in diameter. Heat a dry skillet on medium heat. Grill the flatbreads on each side for 30 to 60 seconds, depending on your preference for crispiness.

Enjoy these flatbreads with any of the savory or sweet soup recipes.

Dill Pickle Bread

Pickles in bread? Yes! This bread is packed with a vibrant tangy flavor. Dill aids digestion by reducing bloating and flatulence, thanks to its fiber content and antacid properties. Adding lacto-fermented vegetables to bread introduces beneficial probiotics, enhancing gut health and digestion. These cultures can help boost the immune system and aid in nutrient absorption. Fermented vegetables contribute a complex flavor profile and add nutritional value, including vitamins, minerals, and enzymes. Sauerkraut's microbiome can help the dough to rise, like a natural sourdough. Additionally, the lactic acid produced during fermentation can act as a natural preservative, potentially extending the bread's shelf life.

Makes about 12 servings

Ingredients:

2½ cups einkorn flour
2 teaspoons baking powder
½ teaspoon baking soda
1 cup yogurt or kefir
½ cup olive oil
1 tablespoon honey
3 tablespoons lacto-fermented dill pickle juice
2 eggs, beaten
1 cup lacto-fermented dill pickles, chopped
1 bunch fresh dill, chopped
1 cup cheddar cheese, grated

(Continued)

Directions:

Grease and flour a 9 × 5-inch loaf pan. In a large bowl, combine the flour, baking powder, and baking soda. Whisk together and set aside.

In a medium bowl, combine yogurt, oil, honey, pickle juice, and eggs. Make a well in the center of the dry ingredients and pour in the yogurt mixture. Stir a few times, and then add the chopped pickles, fresh dill, and grated cheddar cheese. Mix until just combined without overmixing. Spread the batter into the prepared loaf pan. Lightly cover the dough with olive oil. Wrap the loaf pan and allow the dough to rest for an hour or few in the refrigerator. This allows the dough to "cold-rise" and lets the einkorn flour absorb the liquid. Afterward, turn the oven on to 350°F (no preheating) and bake for 50 to 60 minutes, until a toothpick inserted comes out clean. Cool for 15 minutes in the pan before turning out onto a wire rack. Cool completely before slicing.

Enjoy this bread with any of the savory soup recipes.

Savory Parmesan Biscotti

Parmesan cheese is an excellent source of calcium, essential for bone health and preventing osteoporosis. The high-quality protein content supports muscle growth and repair. Additionally, Parmesan contains beneficial fats, such as medium-chain fatty acids (MCTs), which may help lower cholesterol and manage blood sugar levels. Parmesan also contains the probiotic Lactobacillus bacteria, which improves digestion, enhances immune function, and potentially supports gut and vaginal health. Probiotics help maintain a balanced gut microbiome and aid in the production of essential vitamins. Coconut oil offers several potential health benefits, including improved heart health due to its high levels of saturated fats that may increase HDL cholesterol ("good" cholesterol). It can also aid digestion by acting as a prebiotic, supporting healthy gut bacteria. Coconut oil might help boost metabolism due to its medium-chain triglycerides (MCTs). These MCTs are absorbed and metabolized more quickly than long-chain triglycerides found in other oils. Additionally, coconut oil has antimicrobial properties, potentially fighting off harmful bacteria and viruses.

(Continued)

Makes about 12 servings

Ingredients:

2 cups all-purpose gluten-free flour, sifted (see Specialty Ingredients, page 215)
1 teaspoon baking powder
1 teaspoon salt
½ cup freshly grated Parmesan cheese
1 large egg, at room temperature
4 tablespoons coconut oil
1 teaspoon honey
6 tablespoons whole milk

Optional Add-ins:
Fresh herbs
Sliced green olives
Chopped sun-dried tomatoes

Directions:

Preheat the oven to 350°F. Line a large cookie sheet with parchment paper.

In a large bowl, whisk together the flour, baking powder, salt, and Parmesan cheese. Make a well in the dry ingredients, and then add the egg, coconut oil, honey, and milk and add-ins, if using. Mix with a fork until the loose dough is just combined.

Move the mixture onto a flat, floured surface. Knead a few times until a ball forms. If the dough is too sticky, add 1 to 2 tablespoons more flour and knead a bit more.

Roll the dough into a log about 10 inches long. Place the log onto the prepared cookie sheet and bake for 20 minutes. Remove from the oven. Let the log cool for 5 minutes, and then slice into 1-inch pieces. Spread the slices back onto the cookie sheet. Turn the oven up to 400°F. Bake again for 15 minutes or until the center is dry and firm to the touch. The biscotti should be slightly browned. Remove from the oven, let cool on the sheet pan for a few minutes, and then transfer to a wire rack to cool completely.

Enjoy these biscotti with any of the savory soup recipes.

Lentil Sesame Crackers

This gluten- and grain-free recipe is paleo and keto-friendly and great for sensitive diets. Lentils and almonds are both nutrient-dense foods with significant medicinal benefits. Lentils, a legume, are packed with fiber, protein, and complex carbohydrates, making them a heart-healthy choice that can help manage blood sugar levels. They are also rich in folate, iron, and potassium, essential for red blood cell production, oxygen transport, and blood pressure regulation. Almonds, a tree nut, are high in monounsaturated fats, which can help lower bad cholesterol levels and reduce the risk of heart disease. They are also an excellent source of vitamin E, a powerful antioxidant that protects cells from damage and can help heal wounds. Additionally, almonds contain magnesium, which supports nerve and muscle function, and fiber, promoting digestive health.

Makes about 12–16 servings

Ingredients:
1 cup lentils, presoaked,* cooked, and drained
1 cup almond flour
1 teaspoon salt
1 tablespoon honey
3 tablespoons vegetable or coconut oil
1 tablespoon sesame seeds

Optional:
Flaky salt like Maldon (see Specialty Ingredients, page 215)

(Continued)

Directions:

Pulse the lentils in a food processor several times until they start to puree. Add the almond flour, salt, honey, and oil. Pulse the food processor again until a "shaggy" (rough and uneven) dough starts to form. Add the sesame seeds and process until the dough just starts to form into a ball. Be careful not to run the processor too long; keep the sesame seeds mostly whole. Wrap the dough tightly, and pat down to a flattish rough triangle shape. Chill for at least an hour.

After chilling the dough, preheat the oven to 300°F. Remove the dough from the refrigerator, unwrap, and place on a counter. The dough will be sticky, so sprinkle the counter and dough generously with almond flour. Roll out the dough into a 10 × 12-inch triangle and cut into small shapes—rectangles or triangles work well. Occasionally check to be sure the dough can lift off the counter. Carefully transfer dough onto a sheet pan lined with a silicone mat or parchment paper. Sprinkle the tops with flaky salt if desired. Bake for 30 minutes. Let cool completely before removing from the pan.

Enjoy these crackers with any of the savory soup recipes.

---

* Soak lentils overnight, drain off water, and then use fresh water for cooking.

Quinoa Parmesan Crispies

This gluten- and grain-free recipe uses quinoa, a versatile grain-like seed. Quinoa has a complete protein profile, providing all essential amino acids needed by the human body, which makes it valuable for muscle repair and growth. (Few vegetarian protein sources contain complete protein.) Quinoa is also rich in fiber, aiding in digestion, promoting satiety, and helping to regulate blood sugar levels. Quinoa contains antioxidants such as flavonoids that help protect cells from damage and reduce inflammation. Additionally, quinoa has magnesium, iron, and phosphorus, all of which support heart, blood, and bone health, plus many other body functions.

    Parmesan cheese is an excellent source of calcium, essential for bone health and preventing osteoporosis. The high-quality protein content supports muscle growth and repair. Additionally, Parmesan contains beneficial fats, such as medium-chain fatty acids (MCTs), which may help lower cholesterol and manage blood sugar levels. Parmesan also contains the probiotic Lactobacillus bacteria, which improves digestion, enhances immune function, and potentially supports gut and vaginal health. Probiotics help maintain a balanced gut microbiome and aid in the production of essential vitamins. Makes about fifteen 3-inch crackers. Smaller crackers will yield more.

(Continued)

Makes about 12–16 servings

Ingredients:
2 cups quinoa, presoaked,* cooked, cooled, and well-drained
4 ounces of grated or shredded Parmesan

Directions:
Preheat the oven to 350°F. Mix quinoa and Parmesan together. Lightly grease a silicone mat. Mound small scoops of mixture onto the mat. Do not flatten the balls; they will settle with cooking. Bake for 40 minutes. Check occasionally to make sure they don't get too brown. The crackers will be very fragile when removed from the oven, so let them cool completely before handling.

Enjoy these crackers with any of the savory soup recipes.

---

* Soak quinoa overnight, drain off water, and then use fresh water for cooking.

Soup Croutons

Nutritional yeast contains many nutrients and offers numerous health benefits. It's an excellent source of "complete protein," providing all essential amino acids needed by the human body, making it a valuable option for vegetarians and vegans. Packed with B vitamins, including B12, it supports energy production, red blood cell formation, and nerve function. The fiber content, particularly beta-glucan, aids digestion, promotes heart health by reducing cholesterol, and strengthens the immune system. Additionally, nutritional yeast contains antioxidants that combat free radicals, protecting cells from damage.

Try making these with the Dill Pickle Bread (page 197).

Makes about 12–16 servings

Ingredients:
1 teaspoon sea salt
1 teaspoon black pepper
1 teaspoon garlic powder
1 teaspoon onion powder
1 tablespoon fresh herbs, such as rosemary, oregano, or thyme, finely chopped
¼ cup nutritional yeast or Parmesan cheese
1 loaf of bread, cut into 1-inch cubes (see bread recipes in this section)
3 tablespoons olive oil
3 tablespoons melted butter

(Continued)

Directions:

Preheat oven to 400°F. Mix together the spices: salt, pepper, garlic powder, onion powder, fresh herbs, and nutritional yeast. In a large bowl, mix cubed bread with olive oil and melted butter until evenly coated. Spread the cubes on a baking sheet and then sprinkle with the spice mixture. Bake about 10 to 15 minutes, until golden and crispy, flipping halfway through. Let cool completely. Can be stored in an airtight container for up to 2 weeks.

Enjoy these croutons with any of the savory soup recipes.

Almond Shortbread

Almonds offer a wealth of medicinal benefits due to their rich nutrient profile. Packed with monounsaturated fats, they help lower bad cholesterol levels and reduce the risk of heart disease. Almonds are an excellent source of vitamin E, a powerful antioxidant that protects cells from damage and supports immune function. They also contain magnesium, essential for nerve and muscle function, blood sugar control, and bone health. The fiber content aids digestion, promotes satiety, and helps regulate blood sugar levels. Almonds provide protein, copper, and manganese, contributing to various bodily functions. With their combination of healthy fats, vitamins, minerals, and fiber, almonds support overall health and well-being. Additionally, this recipe is gluten-free and grain-free!

People with nut allergies can substitute finely ground pumpkin seeds for the almond flour.

This shortbread is a delicious side for any of the sweet soups in the recipe.

Makes about 12 servings

Ingredients:
1 stick (½ cup) unsalted butter, softened
½ cup maple syrup
½ teaspoon sea salt
1 tablespoon pure vanilla extract
1½ cups almond flour (not almond meal)

(Continued)

Directions:

Mix the butter, maple syrup, and salt together until smooth. Add the vanilla and almond flour. Continue mixing until a smooth dough is formed. Wrap the dough in plastic wrap or parchment and pat into a rough 8-inch square. Chill for at least 1 hour and up to 2 days.

When ready to cook, preheat the oven to 325°F. Remove the dough from the refrigerator and roll out to ½ inch thick. Have extra almond flour on hand if the dough is sticky on the counter. Cut into shortbread circles or squares, about 2 to 3 inches wide. If dough starts to get sticky, return it to the refrigerator for 20 minutes and start again. Bake the shortbread for about 12 to 13 minutes, until golden brown. Allow the shortbread to cool completely before eating.

Enjoy this shortbread with any of the sweet soup recipes.

Specialty Ingredients

The specialty items listed here can be purchased at Whole Foods, Trader Joes, and other natural foods stores. Listed with each item are suggested brands.

- Acadia buckwheat flour: Bouchard Family Farms, ployes.com/buckwheat
- Chili crisp sauce: Fly by Jing, flybyjing.com
- Coconut sugar or sucanat: Wholesome Sweet, wholesomesweet.com
- Corn: Pinole, pinoleblue.com; Masa Harina, masienda.com
- Einkorn flour: Jovial, jovialfoods.com; einkorn.com
- Flaked sea salt: Maldon, maldonsalt.com
- Fresh enoki or shiitake mushrooms, Whole Foods, wholefoodsmarket.com
- Ghee: 4th and Heart, fourthandheart.com
- Gluten-free crackers: Absolutely, absolutelygf.com
- Gluten-free egg noodles: Jovial, jovialfoods.com
- Gluten-free flour: Cup for Cup flour, www.cup4cup.com
- Gluten-free matzo meal: Lakewood Matzo, lakewoodmatzoh.com
- Gluten-free oats: Nature's Path, naturespath.com
- Gluten-free ramen: Lotus Foods, lotusfoods.com
- Healthy cranberry sauce: Whole Foods, wholefoodsmarket.com
- Healthy tomato/vegetable juice: Knudsen, rwknudsen.com
- Kefir: Alexandre Family Farm, alexandrefamilyfarm.com
- Kimchi: Wildbrine, wildbrine.com
- Kombucha: Brew Dr., brewdrkombucha.com
- Mina harissa sauce: Mina, mina.co

- Miso: South River Miso, southrivermiso.com
- Nutritional yeast: Bragg's, bragg.com
- Raw apple cider vinegar: Bragg's, bragg.com
- Raw honey: Really Raw Honey, reallyrawhoney.com
- Sauerkraut: Wildbrine, wildbrine.com
- Sprouted spelt flour: One Degree, onedegreeorganics.com
- Tahini, Artisana, artisanamarket.com
- Tajín seasoning: Tajín, tajin.com
- Tamari: Oshawa Natural Foods, goldminenaturalfoods.com
- Tapioca flour: Arrowhead Mills, arrowheadmills.com

References

Ahmadian, Fereshte, Hassan Mozaffari-Khosravi, Mohammad Hossein Azaraein, Reza Faraji, and Javad Zavar-Reza. 2017. "The Effect of Consumption of Garlic Tablet on Proteins Oxidation Biomarkers in Postmenopausal Osteoporotic Women: A Randomized Clinical Trial." *Electronic Physician* 9 (11): 5670–75. https://doi.org/10.19082/5670.

Ajmera, Rachael. 2023. "6 Nutrition and Health Benefits of Parsnips." Healthline. July 13, 2023. https://www.healthline.com/nutrition/parsnip.

Ballis, Stacey. 2022. "Stock Vs. Broth: What's the Difference?" *Food & Wine*, July 26, 2022. https://www.foodandwine.com/soup/the-difference-between-stock-and-broth.

"The Beneficial Effects of Brassica Vegetables on Human Health." 2012. *PubMed*. 2012. https://pubmed.ncbi.nlm.nih.gov/23631258.

"Benefits of Coconut During Pregnancy." n.d. MamaBix—Special Biscuits for Pregnant and Lactating Women. https://www.mamabix.com/blog/benefits-of-coconut-during-pregnancy.

"Biblical Matzah Recipe." 2020. Natzarim Yahshua Family Fellowship. April 3, 2020. https://natzarimyahshua.org/biblical-matzah-recipe.

Brody, Barbara. 2024. "Pepper Power: Nutrition and Other Benefits." WebMD. October 16, 2024. https://www.webmd.com/diet/peppers-health-benefits.

Camilleri, Michael. 2019. "Leaky Gut: Mechanisms, Measurement and Clinical Implications in Humans." *Gut* 68 (8): 1516–26. https://doi.org/10.1136/gutjnl-2019-318427.

Chavez, Cori. n.d. "Health Benefits of Gluten-Free Diet." Outrageous Baking. https://www.outrageousbaking.com/health-benefits-of-gluten-free-diet.

"Cherries May Help Gout Symptoms." Arthritis Foundation. n.d. https://www.arthritis.org/health-wellness/healthy-living/nutrition/healthy-eating/are-cherries-cure-for-gout.

"Chicken Soup and Other Remedies." n.d. National Endowment for the Humanities. https://www.neh.gov/humanities/2016/fall/feature/chicken-soup-and-other-remedies.

Christofferson, Travis. 2017. *Tripping Over the Truth: How the Metabolic Theory of Cancer Is Overturning One of Medicine's Most Entrenched Paradigms*. Chelsea Green Publishing.

Clemente, Jose C., Luke K. Ursell, Laura Wegener Parfrey, and Rob Knight. 2012. "The Impact of the Gut Microbiota on Human Health: An Integrative View." *Cell* 148 (6): 1258–70. https://doi.org/10.1016/j.cell.2012.01.035.

Cleveland Clinic. 2024. "8 Health Benefits of Cabbage." Cleveland Clinic. June 27, 2024. https://health.clevelandclinic.org/benefits-of-cabbage.

Cleveland Clinic. May 1, 2024. "Low FODMAP Diet." https://my.clevelandclinic.org/health/treatments/22466-low-fodmap-diet.

Crowther, Susan. 2013. *The No Recipe Cookbook: A Beginner's Guide to the Art of Cooking*. Skyhorse Publishing.

Crowther, Susan, and Julie Fallone. 2023. *Pickle & Ferment: Preserve Your Produce & Brew Delicious Probiotic Drinks*. Skyhorse Publishing.

"Cruciferous Vegetables and Cancer Prevention." 2012. Cancer.Gov. June 7, 2012. https://www.cancer.gov/about-cancer/causes-prevention/risk/diet/cruciferous-vegetables-fact-sheet.

Davis, William. 2011. *Wheat Belly: Lose the Wheat, Lose the Weight, and Find Your Path Back to Health*. Rodale.

Dębińska, Anna, and Barbara Sozańska. 2022. "Fermented Food in Asthma and Respiratory Allergies—Chance or Failure?" *Nutrients* 14 (7): 1420. https://doi.org/10.3390/nu14071420.

Devore, Elizabeth E., Jae Hee Kang, Monique M. B. Breteler, and Francine Grodstein. 2012. "Dietary Intakes of Berries and Flavonoids in Relation to Cognitive Decline." *Annals of Neurology* 72 (1): 135–43. https://doi.org/10.1002/ana.23594.

Eastoe, J. E. 1955. "The Amino Acid Composition of Mammalian Collagen and Gelatin." *Biochemical Journal* 61 (4): 589–600. https://doi.org/10.1042/bj0610589.

Endocrine Society. March 31, 2020. "Coconut Oil Reduces Features of Metabolic Syndrome in Obese Females, Animal Study Finds." https://www.endocrine.org/news-and-advocacy/news-room/2020/coconut-oil-reduces-features-of-metabolic-syndrome-in-obese-females-animal-study-finds.

Esme, Mert, Arzu Topeli, Burcu Balam Yavuz, and Murat Akova. 2019. "Infections in the Elderly Critically-Ill Patients." *Frontiers in Medicine* 6 (June). https://doi.org/10.3389/fmed.2019.00118.

Fife, Bruce. 2013. *The Coconut Oil Miracle, 5th Edition*. Penguin.

Gallagher, James. 2015. "'Good Bacteria' Key to Stopping Asthma." BBC News. September 30, 2015. https://www.bbc.com/news/health-34392522.

Gunnars, Kris. 2022. "7 Proven Health Benefits of Dark Chocolate." Healthline. July 13, 2022. https://www.healthline.com/nutrition/7-health-benefits-dark-chocolate.

Hajimonfarednejad, Mahdie, Mohadeseh Ostovar, Fatemeh Sadat Hasheminasab, Mohammad Ali Shariati, Muthu Thiruvengadam, Mohammad Javad Raee, and Mohammad Hashem Hashempur. 2023. "Medicinal Plants for Viral Respiratory Diseases: A Systematic Review on Persian Medicine." *Evidence-Based Complementary and Alternative Medicine* 2023 (1). https://doi.org/10.1155/2023/1928310.

Handwerk, Brian. 2024. "Is Chocolate Actually Good for You?" *Science*, February 12, 2024. https://www.nationalgeographic.com/science/article/chocolate-health-benefits.

Hao, Qiukui, Zhenchan Lu, Bi Rong Dong, Chang Quan Huang, and Taixiang Wu. 2011. "Probiotics for Preventing Acute Upper Respiratory Tract Infections." *Cochrane Database of Systematic Reviews*, August. https://doi.org/10.1002/14651858.cd006895.pub2.

Harvard Gazette. July 22, 2019. "Berries Keep Your Brain Sharp." https://news.harvard.edu/gazette/story/2012/04/berries-keep-your-brain-sharp.

Harvard Health. 2008. "Time for More Vitamin D." September 1, 2008. https://www.health.harvard.edu/staying-healthy/time-for-more-vitamin-d.

Hirsch, Daryl, and Mindi Hirsch. 2024. "45 Best Soups in the World." *2foodtrippers*. December 8, 2024. https://www.2foodtrippers.com/best-soups-in-the-world.

Hobbs, Heather. 2024. "Which Herbs Can Help Reduce Inflammation?" Healthline. October 1, 2024. https://www.healthline.com/health/osteoarthritis/turmeric-and-anti-inflammatory-herbs.

Johansson, Maria A., Ylva M. Sjögren, Jan-Olov Persson, Caroline Nilsson, and Eva Sverremark-Ekström. 2011. "Early Colonization with a Group of Lactobacilli Decreases the Risk for Allergy at Five Years of Age Despite Allergic Heredity." *PLoS ONE* 6 (8): e23031. https://doi.org/10.1371/journal.pone.0023031.

Kandola, Aaron. 2019. "What Are the Health Benefits of Buckwheat?" April 26, 2019. https://www.medicalnewstoday.com/articles/325042.

Katz, Sandor Ellix. 2012. *The Art of Fermentation: An In-depth Exploration of Essential Concepts and Processes from Around the World*. Chelsea Green Publishing.

Kianoush, Sina, Mahdi Balali-Mood, Seyed Reza Mousavi, Valiollah Moradi, Mahmoud Sadeghi, Bita Dadpour, Omid Rajabi, and Mohammad Taghi Shakeri. 2011. "Comparison of Therapeutic Effects of Garlic and d-Penicillamine in Patients with Chronic Occupational Lead Poisoning." *Basic & Clinical Pharmacology & Toxicology* 110 (5): 476–81. https://doi.org/10.1111/j.1742-7843.2011.00841.x.

Klein, Sarah. 2024. "Seaweed: A Tasty, Nutritious Snack." Harvard Health. August 19, 2024. https://www.health.harvard.edu/nutrition/seaweed-a-tasty-nutritious-snack.

Kubala, Jillian. 2020. "9 Surprising Benefits of Curry Powder." Healthline. January 31, 2020. https://www.healthline.com/nutrition/curry-benefits.

Kubala, Jillian. 2024. "Health Benefits of Leeks." Health. February 5, 2024. https://www.health.com/leeks-benefits-8430842.

Leech, Joe. 2023. "10 Delicious Herbs and Spices With Powerful Health Benefits." Healthline. February 15, 2023. https://www.healthline.com/nutrition/10-healthy-herbs-and-spices.

Mar-Solís, Laura M., Adolfo Soto-Domínguez, Luis E. Rodríguez-Tovar, Humberto Rodríguez-Rocha, Aracely García-García, Víctor E. Aguirre-Arzola, Diana E. Zamora-Ávila, Aime J. Garza-Arredondo, and Uziel Castillo-Velázquez. 2021. "Analysis of the Anti-Inflammatory Capacity of Bone Broth in a Murine Model of Ulcerative Colitis." *Medicina* 57 (11): 1138. https://doi.org/10.3390/medicina57111138.

Meléndez-Hevia, Enrique, Patricia De Paz-Lugo, Athel Cornish-Bowden, and María Luz Cárdenas. 2009. "A Weak Link in Metabolism: The Metabolic Capacity for Glycine Biosynthesis Does Not Satisfy the Need for Collagen Synthesis." *Journal of Biosciences* 34 (6): 853–72. https://doi.org/10.1007/s12038-009-0100-9.

Miller, K., et al., (2010) "Reflex Inhibition of Electrically Induced Muscle Cramps in Hypohydrated Humans." *Medicine & Science in Sports & Exercise*. 42 (5), 953-961.

Mumtaz, Shumaila, Shaukat Ali, Rida Khan, Hafiz Abdullah Shakir, Hafiz Muhammad Tahir, Samiara Mumtaz, and Saiqa Andleeb. 2020. "Therapeutic Role of Garlic and Vitamins C and E Against Toxicity Induced by Lead on Various Organs." *Environmental Science and Pollution Research* 27 (9): 8953–64. https://doi.org/10.1007/s11356-020-07654-2.

"New Study Supports Chicken Soup as a Cold Remedy." ScienceDaily. October 19, 2000. https://www.sciencedaily.com/releases/2000/10/001018075252.htm.

NHS. November 29, 2024. "Why 5 a Day?" https://www.nhs.uk/live-well/eat-well/5-a-day/why-5-a-day.

Niland, Benjamin, and Brooks D Cash. 2018. "Health Benefits and Adverse Effects of a Gluten-Free Diet in Non–Celiac Disease Patients." *Gastroenterology & Hepatology*. February 1, 2018. https://www.ncbi.nlm.nih.gov/pmc/articles/PMC5866307.

Okoye, Afy. 2023. "The Best Soups to Kickstart Your Immune System." BlackDoctor.Org. January 6, 2023. https://blackdoctor.org/the-best-soups-to-kickstart-your-immune-system.

Pepper Joe's. March 2, 2021. "9 Amazing Benefits of Eating Hot Peppers That You Must Know." https://pepperjoe.com/blogs/blog/9-amazing-benefits-of-eating-hot-peppers.

Pinole Blue. n.d. "Our Story." https://pinoleblue.com/pages/our-story.

Quin, Shara. 2023. "Citrus Secrets: Unleashing the Connection Between Lemon and Hormones." *Clever Little*. September 15, 2023. https://heycleverlittle.com/blogs/news/citrus-secrets-unleashing-the-connection-between-lemon-and-hormones.

Razak, Meerza Abdul, Pathan Shajahan Begum, Buddolla Viswanath, and Senthilkumar Rajagopal. 2017. "Multifarious Beneficial Effect of

Nonessential Amino Acid, Glycine: A Review." *Oxidative Medicine and Cellular Longevity* 2017 (1). https://doi.org/10.1155/2017/1716701.

"The Role of Gut Health in Respiratory Function: Insights From Functional Medicine." 2025. Rupa Health. January 14, 2025. https://www.rupa health.com/post/the-role-of-gut-health-in-respiratory-function-insights -from-functional-medicine.

Rosa, Damiana D., Manoela M. S. Dias, Łukasz M. Grześkowiak, Sandra A. Reis, Lisiane L. Conceição, and Maria Do Carmo G. Peluzio. 2017. "Milk Kefir: Nutritional, Microbiological and Health Benefits." *Nutrition Research Reviews* 30 (1): 82–96. https://doi.org/10.1017/s0954422416000275.

Sass, Cynthia. 2023. "10 Green Tea Benefits." *Health*. August 28, 2023. https://www.health.com/nutrition/benefits-green-tea.

Schwenk, Donna. 2024. "7 Reasons I Use Einkorn Flour." *Cultured Food Life*. December 16, 2024. https://www.culturedfoodlife.com/7-reasons-i -use-einkorn-flour.

Seidler, Gina Fong. 2024. "Edible Answers to Insomnia?" *Bauman College* (blog). January 8, 2024. https://baumancollege.org/edible-answers -insomnia.

Shubrook, Nicola. "Top 10 Health Benefits of Miso." *Good Food*. October 8, 2024. https://www.bbcgoodfood.com/health/nutrition/health -benefits-miso.

Shubrook, Nicola. 2024a. "Are Cherries Good for You?" *Good Food*. December 7, 2024. https://www.bbcgoodfood.com/health/nutrition /health-benefits-cherries.

Smith, Jamie. 2023. "What Are the Most Healthful Vegetables?" Medical News Today. November 29, 2023. https://www.medicalnewstoday .com/articles/323319.

Spritzler, Franziska. 2018. "8 Evidence-Based Health Benefits of Papaya." Healthline. December 4, 2018. https://www.healthline.com/nutrition /8-proven-papaya-benefits.

Stamets, Paul. n.d. "6 Ways Mushrooms Can Save the World." TED Talk. https://www.ted.com/talks/paul_stamets_6_ways_mushrooms_can _save_the_world.

Streit, Lizzie. 2023. "9 Healthy Beans and Legumes You Should Try." Healthline. June 30, 2023. https://www.healthline.com/nutrition /healthiest-beans-legumes.

"The Surprising Power of Pepper." n.d. https://medericenter.org/resources/dr-pamela-blog.

Thorup, Anne C., Søren Gregersen, and Per B. Jeppesen. 2014. "Ancient Wheat Diet Delays Diabetes Development in a Type 2 Diabetes Animal Model." *The Review of Diabetic Studies* 11 (3–4): 245–57. https://doi.org/10.1900/rds.2014.11.245.

"The Top 10 Amazing Health Benefits of Wild Rice." n.d. Canoe Wild Rice. https://canoewildrice.com/the-top-10-amazing-health-benefits-of-wild-rice/.

US Wellness Meats. "What Is Venison? A Guide to Nutritious Deer Meat." *The Wellness Blog*. July 6, 2023. https://discover.grasslandbeef.com/blog/what-is-venison.

Villanueva, Jose Carlo Miguel M., and Agnes M. Gonzalez-Andaya. 2023. "The Use of Lactobacillus Reuteri as an Adjunct in the Treatment of Children with Newly Diagnosed Asthma in a Tertiary Hospital in the Philippines." *Journal of Medicine University of Santo Tomas* 7 (1): 1080–89. https://doi.org/10.35460/2546-1621.2019-0079.

Wang, Xiao-Jing, Qing Luo, Ai-Sheng Xiong. 2022. "Origin, Evolution, Breeding, and Omics of Apiaceae: A Family of Vegetables and Medicinal Plants." *Horticulture Research* 9 (January). https://doi.org/10.1093/hr/uhac076.

Ware, Megan. 2019. "What Are Superfoods and Why Should You Eat Them?" Medical News Today. January 7, 2019. https://www.medicalnewstoday.com/articles/303079.

WebMD Editorial Contributor. 2024. "Health Benefits of Leeks." WebMD. December 13, 2024. https://www.webmd.com/diet/health-benefits-leeks.

Williams, Jo. 2024. "Top 10 Health Benefits of Fennel." *Good Food*. December 7, 2024. https://www.bbcgoodfood.com/health/nutrition/health-benefits-fennel.

World Health Organization. June 11, 2019. "Cardiovascular Diseases." https://www.who.int/health-topics/cardiovascular-diseases.

Yardley, Katolen. *The Good Living Guide to Natural and Herbal Remedies: Simple Salves, Teas, Tinctures, and More*. 2016. Good Books.

Zhong, Zhi, Micheal D. Wheeler, Xiangli Li, Matthias Froh, Peter Schemmer, Ming Yin, Hartwig Bunzendaul, Blair Bradford, and John J. Lemasters. 2003. "L-Glycine: A Novel Antiinflammatory, Immunomodulatory, and

Cytoprotective Agent." *Current Opinion in Clinical Nutrition & Metabolic Care* 6 (2): 229–40. https://doi.org/10.1097/00075197-200303000-00013.

Zielinski, S. (2013, February 6). "Stone Age Stew? Soup Making May Be Older than We'd Thought." *NPR*. https://www.npr.org/sections/thesalt/2013/02/06/171104410.

About the Authors

Susan Crowther
Susan Crowther writes books on wellness and culinary arts. As a young girl, Susan fell in love with soups while playing Mish Mash, a "culinary jazz" way of cooking, with her mother. Writing this book is the closest she's gotten to realizing her dream of opening a restaurant called The Pinochle Club, featuring "Soups, the World Over." Formerly a chef and teacher, Susan now serves as a writing coach. Susan lives in Vermont with her husband Mark, and her dog Zina.

Julie Fallone
Julie has lived all around the country from New York City to Seattle, Kansas City, Baltimore, and rural Wisconsin in between. She has been a chef, food writer, caterer, recipe tester, and cookbook author. In each place, she has made a home and taken inspiration and influence from its cuisine, art, and culture. Julie says, "Living a creative life is a mandate for me and I can always find ways in all I do to fulfill that. The kitchen is where I am most comfortable and can show my love."

Metric Conversions

If you're accustomed to using metric measurements, use these handy charts to convert the imperial measurements used in this book.

Weight (Dry Ingredients)

1 oz		30 g
4 oz	¼ lb	120 g
8 oz	½ lb	240 g
12 oz	¾ lb	360 g
16 oz	1 lb	480 g
32 oz	2 lb	960 g

Oven Temperatures

Fahrenheit	Celsius	Gas Mark
225°	110°	¼
250°	120°	½
275°	140°	1
300°	150°	2
325°	160°	3
350°	180°	4
375°	190°	5
400°	200°	6
425°	220°	7
450°	230°	8

Volume (Liquid Ingredients)

½ tsp.		2 ml
1 tsp.		5 ml
1 Tbsp.	½ fl oz	15 ml
2 Tbsp.	1 fl oz	30 ml
¼ cup	2 fl oz	60 ml
⅓ cup	3 fl oz	80 ml
½ cup	4 fl oz	120 ml
⅔ cup	5 fl oz	160 ml
¾ cup	6 fl oz	180 ml
1 cup	8 fl oz	240 ml
1 pt	16 fl oz	480 ml
1 qt	32 fl oz	960 ml

Length

¼ in	6 mm
½ in	13 mm
¾ in	19 mm
1 in	25 mm
6 in	15 cm
12 in	30 cm

Index

A
Aleppo pepper
    Lemon Tahini Soup, 148–150
    Shakshuka, 125–127
allspice
    Lacto-Fermented Sauerkraut Stew, 106–108
almond milk
    Chocolate Love, 62–64
almonds
    Savory Wild Rice and Apple Chowder, 154–156
Almond Shortbread, 211–213
apple
    Savory Wild Rice and Apple Chowder, 154–156
arugula
    Green Matzo Ball Soup, 109–112

B
bacon
    Hunter's Stew, 55–57
    turkey
        Lacto-Fermented Sauerkraut Stew, 106–108
barley
    Mushroom Barley Soup, 82–84
Basic Soup Stock, 15–16
Basic Vegetable Stock, 17–19
basil
    Thai Red Curry Noodle Soup, 43–45
    White Bean and Pesto, 76–78
bay leaves
    Basic Soup Stock, 15–16
    Basic Vegetable Stock, 17–19
beans
    black
        Linda's Black Bean Soup, But Better, 113–115
        Pumpkin Chili, 94–96
    cannellini
        White Bean and Pesto, 76–78
    green
        Pesto Pasta Stew, 171–173
        Turkey Dinner in a Bowl, 53–54
    white
        Savory Winter Stew, 134–136
beef
    ground
        Pumpkin Chili, 94–96
beer
    Hunter's Stew, 55–57
Beet Borscht, 73–75
bell pepper
    Happy Baby Soup, 160–162
    Linda's Black Bean Soup, But Better, 113–115
    Pumpkin Chili, 94–96
    Shakshuka, 125–127
    Thai Red Curry Noodle Soup, 43–45
biscotti
    Savory Parmesan Biscotti, 199–201
biscuits
    Herby Biscuits, 190–192
blueberries
    Maple Blueberry Soup, 65–67
bok choy
    Korean Salmon Miso Soup, 157–159
bones
    Basic Soup Stock, 15–16
bread
    Almond Shortbread, 211–213
    Dill Pickle Bread, 196–198
    Easy Yogurt Flatbread, 193–195
    Einkorn Pumpkin Bread, 185–186
    Shakshuka, 125–127
Breathe Well Chicken Soup, 119–121

broccoli
    Green Cleanse Soup, 165–167
broth, 10–13

C
cabbage
    Breathe Well Chicken Soup, 119–121
    Celery Chowder, 177–179
    Savory Winter Stew, 134–136
carrots
    Basic Soup Stock, 15–16
    Basic Vegetable Stock, 17–19
    Breathe Well Chicken Soup, 119–121
    Ginger Carrots with Crispy Chickpeas Soup, 37–39
    Lacto-Fermented Sauerkraut Stew, 106–108
    Lemon Tahini Soup, 148–150
    Linda's Black Bean Soup, But Better, 113–115
    Mushroom Barley Soup, 82–84
    Roasted Lemon Soup, 79–81
    Savory Wild Rice and Apple Chowder, 154–156
    Spanish Lentil, 97–99
    Sunshine Squash Soup, 85–87
    Traditional Chicken Soup, 25–27
    Turkey Dinner in a Bowl, 53–54
cauliflower
    Creamy Cauliflower Soup, 180–182
cayenne
    Green Cleanse Soup, 165–167
    Green Papaya Soup, 103–105
    Linda's Black Bean Soup, But Better, 113–115
    Pumpkin Chili, 94–96
    Sunshine Squash Soup, 85–87
    Traditional Chicken Soup, 25–27
celery
    Basic Soup Stock, 15–16
    Basic Vegetable Stock, 17–19
    Breathe Well Chicken Soup, 119–121
    Celery Chowder, 177–179
    Curried Fish and Chickpea Stew, 131–133
    Fennel and Leek Soup with Thyme, 122–124
    Lemon Tahini Soup, 148–150
    Mushroom Barley Soup, 82–84
    Spanish Lentil, 97–99
    Sunshine Squash Soup, 85–87
    Traditional Chicken Soup, 25–27
    Turkey Dinner in a Bowl, 53–54
Celery Chowder, 177–179
cheese
    cheddar
        Dill Pickle Bread, 196–198
    feta
        Shakshuka, 125–127
        Watermelon Gazpacho, 168–170
    Parmesan
        Parsley Soup with Mini Chicken Meatballs, 46–49
        Parsnip and Kale Soup, 142–144
        Pesto Pasta Stew, 171–173
        Quinoa Parmesan Crispies, 205–207
        Savory Parmesan Biscotti, 199–201
        Soup Croutons, 208–210
        White Bean and Pesto, 76–78
    Sprouted Cornbread Muffins, 187–189
cherries
    Cold Cherry Yogurt, 151–153
chicken
    breast
        Breathe Well Chicken Soup, 119–121
        Chicken and Mushroom with Buckwheat Dumplings, 88–90
        Rice Congee, 100–102
        Traditional Chicken Soup, 25–27
    ground
        Parsley Soup with Mini Chicken Meatballs, 46–49
    Thai Red Curry Noodle Soup, 43–45
    thighs
        Chicken and Mushroom with Buckwheat Dumplings, 88–90
        Traditional Chicken Soup, 25–27
Chicken and Mushroom with Buckwheat Dumplings, 88–90
chicken soup, 8–9
    Breathe Well Chicken Soup, 119–121
    Traditional Chicken Soup, 25–27
chickpeas
    Curried Fish and Chickpea Stew, 131–133
    Ginger Carrots with Crispy Chickpeas Soup, 37–39
    Happy Baby Soup, 160–162
chili
    Pumpkin Chili, 94–96

chili powder
    Chocolate Love, 62–64
    Pumpkin Chili, 94–96
    Shakshuka, 125–127
Chilled Cucumber Avocado Soup, 174–176
chives
    Curried Fish and Chickpea Stew, 131–133
    Green Matzo Ball Soup, 109–112
    Herbed Kefir, 128–130
    Herby Biscuits, 190–192
    Sunshine Squash Soup, 85–87
chocolate
    dark
        Chocolate Love, 62–64
    white
        Maple Blueberry Soup, 65–67
Chocolate Love, 62–64
cilantro
    Ginger Carrots with Crispy Chickpeas Soup, 37–39
    Green Papaya Soup, 103–105
    Linda's Black Bean Soup, But Better, 116
    Sunshine Squash Soup, 85–87
    Thai Red Curry Noodle Soup, 43–45
cinnamon
    Chocolate Love, 62–64
    Einkorn Pumpkin Bread, 185–186
    Maple Blueberry Soup, 65–67
    Pumpkin Chili, 94–96
circulatory system, 68–69
clam juice
    Scallops, Fennel & Parsley Soup, 137–139
cocoa
    Pumpkin Chili, 94–96
coconut
    Chocolate Love, 62–64
coconut milk
    Curried Fish and Chickpea Stew, 131–133
    Green Cleanse Soup, 165–167
    Happy Baby Soup, 160–162
    Thai Red Curry Noodle Soup, 43–45
codfish
    Curried Fish and Chickpea Stew, 131–133
Cold Cherry Yogurt, 151–153
corn
    Sprouted Cornbread Muffins, 187–189
    Triple Corn Soup, 70–72

crackers
    Lentil Sesame Crackers, 202–204
cranberry sauce
    Turkey Dinner in a Bowl, 53–54
cream
    Parsnip and Kale Soup, 142–144
Creamy Cauliflower Soup, 180–182
croutons
    Celery Chowder, 177–179
    Creamy Cauliflower Soup, 180–182
    Fennel and Leek Soup with Thyme, 122–124
    Soup Croutons, 208–210
cucumber
    English
        Chilled Cucumber Avocado Soup, 174–176
        Herbed Kefir, 128–130
        Watermelon Gazpacho, 168–170
cumin
    Creamy Cauliflower Soup, 180–182
    Curried Fish and Chickpea Stew, 131–133
    Ginger Carrots with Crispy Chickpeas Soup, 37–39
    Linda's Black Bean Soup, But Better, 113–115
    Mushroom Barley Soup, 82–84
    Pumpkin Chili, 94–96
    Shakshuka, 125–127
    Sunshine Squash Soup, 85–87
Curried Fish and Chickpea Stew, 131–133
curry, red, Thai-style
    Thai Red Curry Noodle Soup, 43–45
curry powder
    Curried Fish and Chickpea Stew, 131–133
    Sunshine Squash Soup, 85–87

D

digestive system, 92–93
dill
    Dill Pickle Bread, 196–198
    fresh
        Green Matzo Ball Soup, 109–112
        Lacto-Fermented Sauerkraut Stew, 106–108
    Herby Biscuits, 190–192
Dill Pickle Bread, 196–198

E

Easy Yogurt Flatbread, 193–195
edamame
    Korean Salmon Miso Soup, 157–159
egg
    Green Matzo Ball Soup, 109–112
    Harusame (Japanese Glass Noodle Soup), 145–147
    Herbed Kefir, 128–130
    Kefir Mint Soup, 40–42
    Shakshuka, 125–127
Einkorn Pumpkin Bread, 185–186
endocrine system, 140–141

F

Fennel and Leek Soup with Thyme, 122–124
fennel bulb
    Fennel and Leek Soup with Thyme, 122–124
    Scallops, Fennel & Parsley Soup, 137–139
fennel fronds
    Fennel and Leek Soup with Thyme, 122–124
fish
    Curried Fish and Chickpea Stew, 131–133
flatbread
    Easy Yogurt Flatbread, 193–195

G

garlic
    Basic Soup Stock, 15–16
    Basic Vegetable Stock, 17–19
    Beet Borscht, 73–75
    Breathe Well Chicken Soup, 119–121
    Chicken and Mushroom with Buckwheat Dumplings, 88–90
    Creamy Cauliflower Soup, 180–182
    Easy Yogurt Flatbread, 193–195
    Ginger Carrots with Crispy Chickpeas Soup, 37–39
    Green Cleanse Soup, 165–167
    Green Matzo Ball Soup, 109–112
    Green Papaya Soup, 103–105
    Hangover Helper, 60–61
    Hunter's Stew, 55–57
    Lemon Tahini Soup, 148–150
    Linda's Black Bean Soup, But Better, 113–115
    Mushroom Barley Soup, 82–84
    Parsley Soup with Mini Chicken Meatballs, 46–49
    Parsnip and Kale Soup, 142–144
    Pumpkin Chili, 94–96
    Roasted Garlic Soup, 31–33
    Roasted Lemon Soup, 79–81
    Scallops, Fennel & Parsley Soup, 137–139
    Spanish Lentil, 97–99
    Sunshine Squash Soup, 85–87
    Thai Red Curry Noodle Soup, 43–45
    Traditional Chicken Soup, 25–27
    White Bean and Pesto, 76–78
garlic powder
    Ginger Carrots with Crispy Chickpeas Soup, 37–39
    Soup Croutons, 208–210
gazpacho
    Watermelon Gazpacho, 168–170
gelatin, 10–12
ginger
    fresh
        Breathe Well Chicken Soup, 119–121
        Ginger Carrots with Crispy Chickpeas Soup, 37–39
        Green Cleanse Soup, 165–167
        Green Papaya Soup, 103–105
        Korean Salmon Miso Soup, 157–159
        Rice Congee, 100–102
        Sunshine Squash Soup, 85–87
        Thai Red Curry Noodle Soup, 43–45
        Traditional Chicken Soup, 25–27
    powder
        Curried Fish and Chickpea Stew, 131–133
        Harusame (Japanese Glass Noodle Soup), 145–147
Ginger Carrots with Crispy Chickpeas Soup, 37–39
glutamine, 12
glycine, 12
gojuchang
    Shakshuka, 125–127
granola
    Maple Blueberry Soup, 65–67
Green Cleanse Soup, 165–167
Green Matzo Ball Soup, 109–112
Green Papaya Soup, 103–105
Green Tea with Smoked Salmon, 58–59

H

haddock
    Curried Fish and Chickpea Stew, 131–133
Hangover Helper, 60–61
Happy Baby Soup, 160–162
harissa
    Shakshuka, 125–127
Harusame (Japanese Glass Noodle Soup), 145–147
Herbed Kefir, 128–130
Herby Biscuits, 190–192
horseradish
    Hangover Helper, 60–61
    Hunter's Stew, 55–57
hot sauce
    Hangover Helper, 60–61
Hunter's Stew, 55–57

I

immune system, 23–24
integumentary system, 163–164

J

jalapeño
    Chilled Cucumber Avocado Soup, 174–176
    Linda's Black Bean Soup, But Better, 116
    Scallops, Fennel & Parsley Soup, 137–139
    Shakshuka, 125–127
    Watermelon Gazpacho, 168–170

K

kale
    Hunter's Stew, 55–57
    Parsnip and Kale Soup, 142–144
    White Bean and Pesto, 76–78
kefir
    Dill Pickle Bread, 196–198
    Ginger Carrots with Crispy Chickpeas Soup, 37–39
    Green Cleanse Soup, 165–167
    Herbed Kefir, 128–130
    Kefir Mint Soup, 40–42
Kefir Mint Soup, 40–42
kimchi
    Kimchi Jigae (Kimchi Stew), 34–36
Kimchi Jigae (Kimchi Stew), 34–36
kombucha
    Cold Cherry Yogurt, 151–153
    Maple Blueberry Soup, 65–67
    Savory Winter Stew, 134–136
    Scallops, Fennel & Parsley Soup, 137–139
Korean Salmon Miso Soup, 157–159

L

Lacto-Fermented Sauerkraut Stew, 106–108
leeks
    Fennel and Leek Soup with Thyme, 122–124
    Lemon Tahini Soup, 148–150
    Savory Winter Stew, 134–136
    Scallops, Fennel & Parsley Soup, 137–139
lemon
    Scallops, Fennel & Parsley Soup, 137–139
lemon juice
    Chicken and Mushroom with Buckwheat Dumplings, 88–90
    Green Cleanse Soup, 165–167
    Korean Salmon Miso Soup, 157–159
    Parsley Soup with Mini Chicken Meatballs, 46–49
    Traditional Chicken Soup, 25–27
Lemon Tahini Soup, 148–150
lemon zest
    Green Matzo Ball Soup, 109–112
    Maple Blueberry Soup, 65–67
    Parsley Soup with Mini Chicken Meatballs, 46–49
    Parsnip and Kale Soup, 142–144
    White Bean and Pesto, 76–78
lentils
    Spanish Lentil, 97–99
Lentil Sesame Crackers, 202–204
lime juice
    Chilled Cucumber Avocado Soup, 174–176
    Linda's Black Bean Soup, But Better, 116
    Triple Corn Soup, 70–72
    Watermelon Gazpacho, 168–170
Linda's Black Bean Soup, But Better, 113–115

M

Maple Blueberry Soup, 65–67
maple syrup
    Maple Blueberry Soup, 65–67
matzo balls

Green Matzo Ball Soup, 109–112
mint
    Kefir Mint Soup, 40–42
    Parsley Soup with Mini Chicken Meatballs, 46–49
    Watermelon Gazpacho, 168–170
miso
    Green Tea with Smoked Salmon, 58–59
    Korean Salmon Miso Soup, 157–159
    Pesto Pasta Stew, 171–173
    Rice Congee, 100–102
    Roasted Lemon Soup, 79–81
Miso Soup, 28–30
muffins
    Sprouted Cornbread Muffins, 187–189
Mushroom Barley Soup, 82–84
mushrooms
    cremini
        Chicken and Mushroom with Buckwheat Dumplings, 88–90
        Mushroom Barley Soup, 82–84
    enoki
        Kimchi Jigae (Kimchi Stew), 34–36
    shiitake
        Kimchi Jigae (Kimchi Stew), 34–36
        Mushroom Barley Soup, 82–84
mustard powder
    Savory Winter Stew, 134–136

N
nervous system, 50–51
noodles
    Breathe Well Chicken Soup, 119–121
    Harusame (Japanese Glass Noodle Soup), 145–147
    Pesto Pasta Stew, 171–173
nori
    Harusame (Japanese Glass Noodle Soup), 145–147
    Kimchi Jigae (Kimchi Stew), 34–36
    Miso Soup, 28–30

O
oats
    Parsley Soup with Mini Chicken Meatballs, 46–49
olives
    green
        Savory Parmesan Biscotti, 199–201

Spanish Lentil, 97–99
Watermelon Gazpacho, 168–170
onion
    Basic Soup Stock, 15–16
    Basic Vegetable Stock, 17–19
    Beet Borscht, 73–75
    Breathe Well Chicken Soup, 119–121
    Celery Chowder, 177–179
    Creamy Cauliflower Soup, 180–182
    Curried Fish and Chickpea Stew, 131–133
    Ginger Carrots with Crispy Chickpeas Soup, 37–39
    Green Matzo Ball Soup, 109–112
    Green Papaya Soup, 103–105
    Happy Baby Soup, 160–162
    Hunter's Stew, 55–57
    Lacto-Fermented Sauerkraut Stew, 106–108
    Linda's Black Bean Soup, But Better, 113–115
    Mushroom Barley Soup, 82–84
    Parsley Soup with Mini Chicken Meatballs, 46–49
    Parsnip and Kale Soup, 142–144
    Pesto Pasta Stew, 171–173
    Pumpkin Chili, 94–96
    red
        Linda's Black Bean Soup, But Better, 116
        Watermelon Gazpacho, 168–170
    Roasted Garlic Soup, 31–33
    Roasted Lemon Soup, 79–81
    Savory Wild Rice and Apple Chowder, 154–156
    Shakshuka, 125–127
    Spanish Lentil, 97–99
    Sunshine Squash Soup, 85–87
    Thai Red Curry Noodle Soup, 43–45
    Traditional Chicken Soup, 25–27
    Turkey Dinner in a Bowl, 53–54
    White Bean and Pesto, 76–78
onion powder
    Soup Croutons, 208–210
orange juice
    Cold Cherry Yogurt, 151–153
    Maple Blueberry Soup, 65–67
Orange Salsa, 116
    Linda's Black Bean Soup, But Better, 113–115

orange zest
  Chocolate Love, 62–64
  Linda's Black Bean Soup, But Better, 113–115
oregano
  Linda's Black Bean Soup, But Better, 113–115
  Roasted Garlic Soup, 31–33
  Soup Croutons, 208–210
  Traditional Chicken Soup, 25–27

P
papaya
  Green Papaya Soup, 103–105
paprika
  Ginger Carrots with Crispy Chickpeas Soup, 37–39
  Lemon Tahini Soup, 148–150
  Mushroom Barley Soup, 82–84
  Shakshuka, 125–127
  smoked
    Pumpkin Chili, 94–96
    Shakshuka, 125–127
    Spanish Lentil, 97–99
parsley
  Beet Borscht, 73–75
  Chicken and Mushroom with Buckwheat Dumplings, 88–90
  Chilled Cucumber Avocado Soup, 174–176
  Curried Fish and Chickpea Stew, 131–133
  Green Matzo Ball Soup, 109–112
  Green Tea with Smoked Salmon, 58–59
  Mushroom Barley Soup, 82–84
  Parsley Soup with Mini Chicken Meatballs, 46–49
  Roasted Lemon Soup, 79–81
  Scallops, Fennel & Parsley Soup, 137–139
  Shakshuka, 125–127
  Traditional Chicken Soup, 25–27
  Turkey Dinner in a Bowl, 53–54
Parsley Soup with Mini Chicken Meatballs, 46–49
parsnip
  Lacto-Fermented Sauerkraut Stew, 106–108
Parsnip and Kale Soup, 142–144
pears
  Savory Winter Stew, 134–136

peas
  Breathe Well Chicken Soup, 119–121
  Pesto Pasta Stew, 171–173
peppercorns
  Basic Soup Stock, 15–16
  Basic Vegetable Stock, 17–19
pesto
  Pesto Pasta Stew, 171–173
Pesto Pasta Stew, 171–173
pickle juice
  Dill Pickle Bread, 196–198
pickles
  Dill Pickle Bread, 196–198
pineapple
  Chilled Cucumber Avocado Soup, 174–176
pine nuts
  White Bean and Pesto, 76–78
poblano peppers
  Sprouted Cornbread Muffins, 187–189
pork
  ground
    Kimchi Jigae (Kimchi Stew), 34–36
  loin
    Linda's Black Bean Soup, But Better, 113–115
potatoes
  Celery Chowder, 177–179
  Green Matzo Ball Soup, 109–112
  Hunter's Stew, 55–57
  Lacto-Fermented Sauerkraut Stew, 106–108
  red
    Beet Borscht, 73–75
    Parsnip and Kale Soup, 142–144
    Roasted Garlic Soup, 31–33
    Scallops, Fennel & Parsley Soup, 137–139
    Sunshine Squash Soup, 85–87
  sweet
    Happy Baby Soup, 160–162
    Turkey Dinner in a Bowl, 53–54
Pumpkin Chili, 94–96
pumpkin puree
  Einkorn Pumpkin Bread, 185–186
  Pumpkin Chili, 94–96
pumpkin seeds
  Green Cleanse Soup, 165–167
  Sunshine Squash Soup, 85–87

Q
Quinoa Parmesan Crispies, 205–207

R
respiratory system, 117–118
rice
    brown
        Lemon Tahini Soup, 148–150
        Roasted Lemon Soup, 79–81
        Curried Fish and Chickpea Stew, 131–133
        Green Tea with Smoked Salmon, 58–59
        Kefir Mint Soup, 40–42
        Kimchi Jigae (Kimchi Stew), 34–36
        Rice Congee, 100–102
Rice Congee, 100–102
Roasted Garlic Soup, 31–33
Roasted Lemon Soup, 79–81
rosemary
    Breathe Well Chicken Soup, 119–121
    Hunter's Stew, 55–57
    Parsnip and Kale Soup, 142–144
    Soup Croutons, 208–210
    Traditional Chicken Soup, 25–27
    Turkey Dinner in a Bowl, 53–54

S
salmon
    Korean Salmon Miso Soup, 157–159
    smoked
        Green Tea with Smoked Salmon, 58–59
salsa
    Linda's Black Bean Soup, But Better, 113–115
sauerkraut
    Lacto-Fermented Sauerkraut Stew, 106–108
sausage
    Italian turkey
        Savory Winter Stew, 134–136
Savory Parmesan Biscotti, 199–201
Savory Wild Rice and Apple Chowder, 154–156
Savory Winter Stew, 134–136
scallions
    Green Papaya Soup, 103–105
    Harusame (Japanese Glass Noodle Soup), 145–147
    Kimchi Jigae (Kimchi Stew), 34–36
    Korean Salmon Miso Soup, 157–159
    Miso Soup, 28–30
scallops
    Scallops, Fennel & Parsley Soup, 137–139
Scallops, Fennel & Parsley Soup, 137–139
seaweed
    Harusame (Japanese Glass Noodle Soup), 145–147
    Kimchi Jigae (Kimchi Stew), 34–36
    Miso Soup, 28–30
sesame oil
    Harusame (Japanese Glass Noodle Soup), 145–147
sesame seeds
    Green Tea with Smoked Salmon, 58–59
    Korean Salmon Miso Soup, 157–159
    Lentil Sesame Crackers, 202–204
Shakshuka, 125–127
shallot
    Chicken and Mushroom with Buckwheat Dumplings, 88–90
    Rice Congee, 100–102
    Triple Corn Soup, 70–72
shortbread
    Almond Shortbread, 211–213
skin, 163–164
Soup Croutons, 208–210
Spanish Lentil, 97–99
spinach
    Green Cleanse Soup, 165–167
    Green Matzo Ball Soup, 109–112
    Happy Baby Soup, 160–162
    Pesto Pasta Stew, 171–173
    Spanish Lentil, 97–99
Sprouted Cornbread Muffins, 187–189
squash
    butternut
        Sunshine Squash Soup, 85–87
        Turkey Dinner in a Bowl, 53–54
star anise
    Traditional Chicken Soup, 25–27
stock, 10–13
    Basic Soup Stock, 15–16
    chicken
        Breathe Well Chicken Soup, 119–121
        Chicken and Mushroom with Buckwheat Dumplings, 88–90

Ginger Carrots with Crispy Chickpeas Soup, 37–39
Kefir Mint Soup, 40–42
Linda's Black Bean Soup, But Better, 113–115
Parsley Soup with Mini Chicken Meatballs, 46–49
Rice Congee, 100–102
Savory Winter Stew, 134–136
Scallops, Fennel & Parsley Soup, 137–139
Thai Red Curry Noodle Soup, 43–45
Traditional Chicken Soup, 25–27
Turkey Dinner in a Bowl, 53–54

fish
Scallops, Fennel & Parsley Soup, 137–139

Hangover Helper, 60–61
Harusame (Japanese Glass Noodle Soup), 145–147
Hunter's Stew, 55–57
Kimchi Jigae (Kimchi Stew), 34–36
Lacto-Fermented Sauerkraut Stew, 106–108
Mushroom Barley Soup, 82–84
Pumpkin Chili, 94–96
Roasted Garlic Soup, 31–33
Spanish Lentil, 97–99

turkey
Turkey Dinner in a Bowl, 53–54

vegetable
Beet Borscht, 73–75
Celery Chowder, 177–179
Creamy Cauliflower Soup, 180–182
Curried Fish and Chickpea Stew, 131–133
Fennel and Leek Soup with Thyme, 122–124
Green Cleanse Soup, 165–167
Green Matzo Ball Soup, 109–112
Happy Baby Soup, 160–162
Korean Salmon Miso Soup, 157–159
Lemon Tahini Soup, 148–150
Miso Soup, 28–30
Parsnip and Kale Soup, 142–144
Pesto Pasta Stew, 171–173
Roasted Lemon Soup, 79–81
Savory Wild Rice and Apple Chowder, 154–156

Shakshuka, 125–127
Sunshine Squash Soup, 85–87
White Bean and Pesto, 76–78

strawberries
Chocolate Love, 62–64

Sunshine Squash Soup, 85–87

T
tahini
Ginger Carrots with Crispy Chickpeas Soup, 37–39
Lemon Tahini Soup, 148–150
Roasted Lemon Soup, 79–81

Tajín seasoning
Chilled Cucumber Avocado Soup, 174–176

tamari
Celery Chowder, 177–179
Green Tea with Smoked Salmon, 58–59
Happy Baby Soup, 160–162
Harusame (Japanese Glass Noodle Soup), 145–147
Kimchi Jigae (Kimchi Stew), 34–36
Korean Salmon Miso Soup, 157–159
Rice Congee, 100–102
Thai Red Curry Noodle Soup, 43–45

tarragon
Celery Chowder, 177–179
Herbed Kefir, 128–130

tea
green
Green Tea with Smoked Salmon, 58–59

Thai Red Curry Noodle Soup, 43–45

thyme
Basic Soup Stock, 15–16
Basic Vegetable Stock, 17–19
Breathe Well Chicken Soup, 119–121
Fennel and Leek Soup with Thyme, 122–124
Lemon Tahini Soup, 148–150
Soup Croutons, 208–210
Spanish Lentil, 97–99
Traditional Chicken Soup, 25–27

tofu
Harusame (Japanese Glass Noodle Soup), 145–147
Kimchi Jigae (Kimchi Stew), 34–36
Miso Soup, 28–30

tomato
    Curried Fish and Chickpea Stew, 131–133
    Herbed Kefir, 128–130
    Hunter's Stew, 55–57
    Mushroom Barley Soup, 82–84
    Pumpkin Chili, 94–96
    Shakshuka, 125–127
    Spanish Lentil, 97–99
    sun-dried
        Savory Parmesan Biscotti, 199–201
    Sunshine Squash Soup, 85–87
tomato juice
    Hangover Helper, 60–61
tortillas
    Triple Corn Soup, 70–72
Traditional Chicken Soup, 25–27
Triple Corn Soup, 70–72
turkey
    bacon
        Lacto-Fermented Sauerkraut Stew, 106–108
    ground
        Parsley Soup with Mini Chicken Meatballs, 46–49
        Pumpkin Chili, 94–96
    Turkey Dinner in a Bowl, 53–54
Turkey Dinner in a Bowl, 53–54
turmeric
    Breathe Well Chicken Soup, 119–121
    Creamy Cauliflower Soup, 180–182
    Ginger Carrots with Crispy Chickpeas Soup, 37–39
    Green Cleanse Soup, 165–167
    Sunshine Squash Soup, 85–87
    Triple Corn Soup, 70–72

V

venison
    Hunter's Stew, 55–57
vinegar
    apple cider
        Beet Borscht, 73–75
        Roasted Garlic Soup, 31–33
        Traditional Chicken Soup, 25–27

    red wine
        Linda's Black Bean Soup, But Better, 113–115
    white rice
        Kimchi Jigae (Kimchi Stew), 34–36

W

walnuts
    White Bean and Pesto, 76–78
Watermelon Gazpacho, 168–170
White Bean and Pesto, 76–78
wine
    red
        Linda's Black Bean Soup, But Better, 113–115
    white
        Scallops, Fennel & Parsley Soup, 137–139
Worcestershire sauce
    Hangover Helper, 60–61
    Hunter's Stew, 55–57

Y

yeast, nutritional
    Ginger Carrots with Crispy Chickpeas Soup, 37–39
    Soup Croutons, 208–210
yogurt
    Beet Borscht, 73–75
    Dill Pickle Bread, 196–198
    Ginger Carrots with Crispy Chickpeas Soup, 37–39
    Greek
        Cold Cherry Yogurt, 151–153
        Easy Yogurt Flatbread, 193–195
        Maple Blueberry Soup, 65–67
    Green Cleanse Soup, 165–167
    Sunshine Squash Soup, 85–87
vanilla
    Chocolate Love, 62–64

Z

zucchini
    Pesto Pasta Stew, 171–173